Book 4, The Pet Bereavement Series

My Cat Has Died: What Do I Do?

Making Decisions and Healing the Trauma of Pet Loss

Wendy Van de Poll, MS, CEOL

ISBN: 978-0-9973756-3-3

DISCLAIMER

If you are ever feeling like you can no longer function with your life, become suicidal, and any of the normal grief feelings have become extreme for you, then that is considered unhealthy grief. This is the time to call your hospital, medical practitioner, psychologist, or other health care provider that is trained to help you. Do not isolate yourself if you are experiencing unhealthy grief. Get the professional help that you require.

THANK YOU!

Thank you for purchasing *My Cat Has Died: What Do I Do?*
To show my appreciation, I'm offering this special gift to
support your journey because I am compassionately
dedicated to helping you...my valued reader.

Healing Cat Loss Meditation.mp3 will help calm the
chaos and anxiety that you may be experiencing.

To Download Your **FREE GIFT**

Healing Cat Loss Meditation.mp3

Please Go To:
www.centerforpetlossgrief.com/book-4-gift-sign-up-page/

This book is dedicated all the felines that have yet to find their forever homes.

It is my wish that you find your way to rescue the hearts of cat-lovers who read this book and are coping with the loss of their feline companions.

Contents

Introduction

You are at home, sitting on the couch, and within a split second you are aware of something very unusual and different. Something is missing and you are feeling deeply alone and your heart is empty. This feeling is confusing to you and gets stronger with every moment—until reality hits you!

Your cat is not there. Your cat is not snuggled on your lap purring as you shower her with love and compassion. You cat is not there to listen to you as you share your daily adventures. Your cat isn't pawing at your socks and grooming on her pillow.

Realistically, what are you going to do? She is your best friend, and you couldn't imagine what life would be like without her sweet meows, gentle nuzzles, and heart-vibrating purrs that filled your soul with delight. You wanted more time with her, and you wish she were still with you.

You ask yourself, "What am I going to do?"

The answer to this question—and the good news—is what I'll be sharing in this book. I'm offering tools to support you through your grief and guide you on how to deal with all the changes that you are going to experience immediately after the death of your cat as well as support on how to prepare for the future. In this book, I supply you with options for ways to rescue yourself from the potentially overwhelming pet loss emotions when your cat is no longer physically with you.

This book is for you if you if your cat has died and you are experiencing grief, having difficulty making important decisions, and you want to do something special to not forget the life you shared with your cat.

My Cat Has Died: What Do I Do? Making Decisions and Healing the Trauma of Pet Loss has been written to give you options and tools for navigating your personal journey through this raw and challenging time, a time filled with so many emotions and unexpected experiences. It is here as a handbook to keep with you as a constant guide to offer support in this particular phase of losing your cat.

My Cat Has Died: What Do I Do? Making Decisions and Healing the Trauma of Pet Loss will help you gain a deeper spiritual understanding of why your cat was in your life and will show you that even though your cherished feline is not physically with you, your special and unique spiritual relationship with them will continue to grow. You will learn ways to talk to your cat, so you can experience their presence never completely leaving you.

Something special I'm offering you that I've not found in other pet grief books are contemplation questions. At the end of each chapter, you will find three *Contemplation Questions,* designed to help you proceed even more profoundly and personally in your journey. Additionally, I'm offering a free, downloadable Healing Cat Loss Meditation.mp3 to help you calm the chaos and anxiety that you may be experiencing. When you become a dynamic participant in managing your grief, the changes and growth that you experience become very personal.

With years of experience in supporting people as their cats go from the physical to the spiritual realm I have gained a tremendous amount of wisdom and knowledge concerning the soul of the cat. Our cats have a unique view of the world and of us. And when we listen to their voices, they can have a profound effect on the way we as humans approach life.

Along with my personal experiences with cats, plus being a certified end-of-life and pet loss grief coach (CEOL), as well as a licensed massage therapist for humans, horses, hounds, and, at times, cats, I have helped countless people around the world to feel safe with their feelings of grief and have a compassionate outlet to express what they are feeling.

People who feel alone with their feelings of grief when their cats have reached the end of life have found support from the suggestions and information in this helpful book.

Sasha, whose cat Louie suffered kidney failure, explained—

This book is written with kindness and love, which is just what I needed when going through such a difficult time with Louie. I could dive right in and get the support and guidance I needed. There in the book are Wendy's words to help you understand and deal with feelings of grief and to help you reflect upon your time with your cat. This book helps ensure you are doing everything to celebrate their life and to manage your own grief over your loss. Her words will help you heal.

The case studies showed me that others have been through what I am going through, and they found a way to live through it and even experience moments of joy. I also liked the "Contemplation Questions" at the end of each chapter, which gave me a chance to explore my feelings and understand that they are normal for me. One of the toughest things about saying good-bye to Louie was knowing when would be the right time to let go. Wendy helped me with this and provided guidance on final-day preparation. This is such a difficult subject, but Wendy writes with apparent understanding and great compassion.

I promise you that when you read and follow the tips in this book, you will feel like you have acquired a new best friend who totally gets what you are going through. And I promise it will be your first-aid kit that will give you solutions to some of the most difficult decisions and situations that you will experience.

Please don't be the person who goes through this difficult time of loss alone. Be the person who actively takes death by the hand. Be the person who can make sound decisions on how to honor your cat during this special time. And be the person who looks at the pet loss grief journey not as an opportunity to fear death but as a journey to learn, love, grow, and heal.

The book that you are about to read will help you create a compassionate, respectful, healthy, and loving journey for yourself, all the while honoring your beloved cat, during this tough, yet unique, time.

Remember—you never have to feel alone with your pet loss grief again!

LIFE WITHOUT YOUR CAT BEGINS: SECTION ONE

No one ever told me that grief feels like fear.

—C.S. Lewis

1. Discovering Your Grief

You don't need anyone telling you that the life you shared with your cat was special and unique! You had moments of deep and enduring love that filled your heart on a daily basis. The memories that you value are what will keep you connected to your cat forever.

Yet, right now everything is unusual and new for you. Your cat is no longer physically with you, and you are noticing some very uncomfortable feelings that you are unsure of. Your emotions may be creating chaos in your life—you may be feeling extreme anxiety or even depression. You may be unsure of what to do next.

Many of my clients ask me, "Does my sadness over the loss of my cat ever go away?" I would like to answer yes, but to be perfectly frank, the answer is no. However, by understanding what grief is and by employing the great tools and support that I offer you in this book, you are going to find that you are not alone. You will be able to navigate this tough journey with respect, forgiveness, and love—for both your cat and yourself.

If you read the third book in this series, *My Cat Is Dying: What Do I Do? Navigating the Emotions, Decisions, and Options for Healing*, you read a lot about the characteristics of normal grief. Although there are many similarities with experiencing grief while your cat is alive, your grief will change after they are no longer in your life.

As you continue your journey of grief or are just starting out with pet loss, I encourage you to consider this book as a trusted companion and support tool that will guide you and walk the journey of pet loss grief with you.

I will help you understand what normal grief is and how you can begin to cope with it in this chapter.

Normal and Healthy Grief

If you are feeling hopeless right now because you don't know whom to talk to, how to get help, or whom to get help from—you are experiencing normal grief. This chapter will help you understand and support this uncomfortable but normal feeling.

If you are experiencing anger that your furry companion died or if you are feeling guilty, depressed, numb, or even shock—you are experiencing normal pet grief, and the tools in this book will help you process those feelings so that you will be able to appreciate and then celebrate the life you had with your cat.

Once you understand what normal grief is and what the expectations are for you, your journey will become different—and more manageable.

Case Study —Kris and Lily

Kris was devastated that she had to euthanize her nine-year-old tabby named Lily. When she called me, it was 4 weeks since Lily had died. Kris was talking really fast, couldn't sit down, and she hadn't slept, eaten, or talked to anyone. She was beginning to isolate herself from her friends and family.

During our first few conversations, Kris was so distraught that she wasn't even able to form complete sentences when explaining the situation to me. She was bouncing from episode to episode, all the while expressing bouts of anger, anxiety, and sadness. Then at times, she was completely silent because she didn't know how she felt.

Your might find this interesting—Kris was having a healthy reaction to her loss. No, Kris's grief was not easy or comfortable, but it was necessary and healthy for her to experience.

I know that sounds strange, but this is how grief works: the fact that Kris could outwardly express herself to someone, who was nonjudgmental and could listen to what she had to say without adding advice or suggestions, is what helped Kris understand and cope with her grief, which, in turn, made her grief experience less fear-and anxiety-ridden.

Just to clarify further, even though Kris's grief was normal, that didn't mean it was easy or short-lived. Kris was feeling weird about her feelings and was not comfortable with what was going on in her mind, in her body, and with her spiritual beliefs. And this is part of the normal, but unpleasant, grief experience.

Kris also suffered from a huge amount of guilt after Lily died. She felt guilty about not doing more for Lily when she was alive. Lily loved chasing the laser, and Kris spent a lot of time on the computer. When Lily requested playtime, Kris often ignored these requests. Again, feeling such guilt is excruciating but also—normal.

During our conversation, I encouraged Kris to talk about everything that she was feeling and going through—all the feelings that were driving her crazy and how she was going to begin to share this news with others.

The result—Kris began to make sense of the myriad of feelings and physical sensations she was experiencing. She began to understand that what she was going through was very difficult but also—normal.

Plus, she learned that her original expectation—that she could avoid feeling grief—was not realistic. When this expectation changed and she realized that grief was healthy, she felt much better.

Over the course of our working together in my Rescue Joy from Pet Loss Grief program, Kris learned that her experiences of pet grief were difficult and uncomfortable but, at the same time, normal, healthy, and special.

By understanding her feelings and accepting those crazy thoughts, sensations, and spiritual upheavals, she began to walk the journey of losing the physical Lily with respect for herself. This, in turn, gave her the direction and focus she needed to be present for the possibilities of a continued relationship with Lily on a spiritual level.

When our conversation for that day ended, Kris wasn't free from feeling grief. Yet, she had more strength and grounding to move forward to contemplate her next moment in this special journey.

Element 1 — Normal and Necessary

What Kris's story demonstrates is that the first thing about grief over the death of your cat is to know that what you are feeling and thinking, though uncomfortable and difficult, is also normal and healthy. Grief is necessary, so it is critical that you let your feelings happen.

If you stuff grief down, so many detrimental things can happen to your health and well-being. Stuffing grief down will affect how you live—in a negative way—from the day your cat dies, to how you will mourn, and to how you begin to move forward.

In fact, if you stuff your feelings down, your normal grief feelings can become unhealthy and result in unhealthy actions. We will talk about unhealthy grief later in this chapter.

Normal Grief Feelings — A List

Here are some normal feelings of pet grief that you may experience now or later in your journey.

- *Physical* ~ crying, sobbing, wailing, numbness, dry mouth, nausea, tightness in the chest, restlessness, fatigue, sleep disturbance, appetite disturbance, dizziness, fainting, or shortness of breath

- *Intellectual* ~ sense of unreality, inability to concentrate, feeling preoccupied with the loss, hallucinations concerning the loss, a sense that time is passing very slowly, or a desire to rationalize feelings about the loss

- *Emotional* ~ anger, depression, guilt, anxiety, relief, irritability, desire to blame others for the loss, self-doubt, lowered self-esteem, feeling overwhelmed, or feeling out of control, hopeless, or helpless

- *Social* ~ feelings of isolation or alienation, feeling rejected by others, or reluctance to ask for help

- *Spiritual* ~ feeling angry at your deity after your cat died and blaming them for the loss, or even bargaining to try and get your cat back.

A Life of Its Own

As you can see, normal grief is varied and expansive. The thing about grief is that it has a life of its own. What this means is that you can be going through a quiet period of your journey when you are feeling relatively good. Then something happens, and it triggers intense, and perhaps unexpected, feelings of pet grief.

I am here to tell you to let this happen. Let yourself feel what you are going through. Let those feelings rage. Let your tears flow. It's healthy and necessary.

Abnormal Grief Feelings

Yet, if you are ever feeling like you can no longer function with your life or if you become suicidal and any of the normal grief feelings become extreme, then that is considered unhealthy grief. This is the time to call your hospital, medical practitioner, psychologist, or a healthcare provider that is trained to help you. Do not isolate yourself if you are experiencing unhealthy grief. Get the professional help that you require.

Element 2 — Reach Out

In addition to recognizing your normal grief feelings, a second essential component for navigating your pet grief journey is to reach out to someone else, as Kris did. Look for someone who will listen to every word of your conversation with respect and compassion, and share your grief experience with this person. In doing this, you will feel better about what you are going through, you will feel supported, and you will come to better understand your own grief.

Element 3 — Spend Time with Your Memories

Spend time with your memories. Look at photos, write down special moments, and reflect on the intense love that you shared with your furry friend. By doing this, you can calm your raging emotions and begin to develop a different kind of relationship with your cat, one which we will talk about more in chapters 12, 13, and 15.

Element 4 — Know Your Grief Feelings

Also, it is important to be familiar with your unique grief feelings. Everyone grieves differently, so get to know your own grief. Your feelings are going to be with you every single day. When I help my clients understand their grief, it becomes less of a burden or something to fear. You are going to be spending a lot of time with your feelings over the next few days, months, and even years, so it is important that you come to know those feelings and not fear them.

Spend some time responding to the three *Contemplation Questions* at the end of this chapter. These questions will help guide you to recognize your own unique feelings of normal pet grief that you are experiencing.

Chapter Wrap-Up

Losing your cherished cat is extremely difficult. Your cat was your constant companion. You both loved each other unconditionally.

The first twenty-four hours (more on this in chapter 5) is one of the most difficult transitions to experience.

Try to understand your unique feelings of grief and spend time just being in the moment by breathing and preparing yourself for the journey to come. Revisit the four elements I've given you in this chapter and begin to internalize and act upon them. Respond to the chapter's *Contemplation Questions* to help you manage your normal, but uncomfortable, feelings of grief.

In chapter 2, I am going to teach you the seven stages of grief that you may or may not experience in full. With each of these stages, I am going to give you examples of what you can expect from yourself as well as from other people.

Chapter 1 Contemplation Questions

1. What feelings of grief do you have now?

2. How are you dealing with these feelings? Can you make a list of your feelings, arranging them from the most intense feelings first, down to the least charged?

3. If you have any abnormal feelings of grief, write down your healthcare practitioner's contact information and have it readily available.

2. Identifying Your Stages of Grief and Loss

As I shared in the first chapter, grief has a life of its own. If you are feeling sad, angry, or like your heart is raw with pain—please understand that this is absolutely okay.

We all experience these feelings in different ways and at different times. By remembering that your grief is unique and special to the relationship that you had with your treasured cat, you can be ready with less confusion or difficulty for your future stages of grief.

Keep in mind there is more to your journey of coping than the fact that your cat is no longer physically in your life.

Pet loss grief actually has seven identifiable stages. By understanding these seven stages of grief, your disordered emotions and possible shock about what you are now faced with can change, so you can hopefully feel less stress as you move through these stages.

Learning which stage of pet loss grief you are experiencing is extremely helpful to your coping and healing journey. You can gain compassion and respect for your own process, both of which are vital to finding joy after suffering so much intense grief from your loss.

Living without your cat is ridiculously difficult. The shock, horror, and unrelenting pain can easily inhibit you from taking care of yourself. By exploring the stages of grief, you can begin to learn self-compassion and gain a needed understanding of your journey.

No matter what you are experiencing after the death of your cat, one of the most important things to remember is to cherish the life you had with them. The memories you have are beautiful, and the stages of grief that you are experiencing will only have a positive effect on your continued spiritual relationship with your cat.

The grief that you are feeling right now is perfect, so please be kind to yourself and not expect anything more or anything less. It is there, and it's not going to go away. Yet, it will change as time progresses.

The Seven Stages of Grief

It is extremely helpful to know not only what normal grief is but also what the normal stages of grief are.

Dr. Elisabeth Kubler-Ross was a pioneer in the hospice movement. While she wasn't a pet grief person, what she discovered can be applied to the journey of pet grief.

In 1969, in her book *On Death and Dying*, Dr. Kubler-Ross made the five steps of grief and/or death well-known. The following five steps cover the stages of grieving for the death of a loved one:

1. Denial

2. Anger

3. Bargaining

4. Depression

5. Acceptance

These five stages became very popular and are recognized widely, mostly as they apply to the dying process. However, people working in this field began to expand on Kubler-Ross's various philosophies and standards. Currently, there are seven stages of grief:

1. Shock and Denial

2. Pain and Guilt

3. Anger and Bargaining

4. Depression, Reflection, and Loneliness

5. Adjustment to Life

6. Your New Normal

7. Acceptance and Hope

Over the years my clients had told me that this information is valuable and helps prepare them every day to live more fully and have hope for the future.

Keep in mind that since your journey is yours, you may not experience all of these stages as your daily pet loss progresses. Yet you may. Whatever you experience is normal, so be compassionate with yourself for what you are going through. Never compare your experience to someone else's.

Case Study — Melissa, Ra, and the Seven Stages

Melissa, a client of mine, experienced all seven stages of grief. She and I started working together twelve months after Ra died. When Melissa recalled her feelings and actions through our conversations, she felt much better and more in control of what she had experienced and was currently experiencing.

Even still, Melissa was confused and worried because she continued to break down in tears whenever she thought of getting another cat. Her best friend was telling her that twelve months was too long to still be feeling sad and that she should be over it by now (the length of the grieving period is something we'll address in chapter 5).

Stage One: Shock and Denial

As we worked together, Melissa began to understand why she felt the unshakable feelings of trauma and not believing that Ra had died. Melissa recalled that during the first 24 hours of being alone without Ra, she felt totally in shock and nauseous. She remembered checking under the bed countless times throughout the night.

Melissa was distressed, upset, and in denial that Ra wasn't with her any longer, even twelve months later. She said to me during one of our calls, "This did not happen, and I know Ra will come back to me."

Stage Two: Pain and Guilt

Melissa was feeling intense torment and sorrow, so much so that she suffered from headaches since Ra had died. I assured her that her feelings were common and in accordance with the second stage of grief.

When this information started to settle in and become more accepted, Melissa understood her feelings better. When she began to forgive herself for any guilt she had, her headaches started to go away.

Stage Three: Anger and Bargaining

When Melissa got angry, she was insistent on blaming herself and her spiritual deities. She told me when we began working together that at times she still bargained with them and asked them to give her directions on to bring Ra back, alive.

Melissa told me she went through a stage where she was furious. Melissa explained, "My anger was so intense that I had myself believing that I could bring Ra back to life by bargaining and convincing my guides that it was possible. When you helped me realize that others experience this and it is common, I didn't feel so weird about my anger and expectations."

Stage Four: Depression, Reflection, and Loneliness

When Melissa and I started to work together, she was beginning to understand that anger and bargaining were part of the journey. Plus, she was also experiencing some depression and loneliness.

Whenever she started to think about Ra and the times that they had had together, she felt sad and very lonely. She told me, "Everyone around me keeps saying that I am grieving long enough. I don't have anyone that I can talk to. I feel like I have to do this alone."

As we continued to work together, Melissa began to understand that her feelings of loneliness were part of the grief process, especially when she reflected on the past. After she understood that her reflections triggered loneliness, she was able to experience her feelings in a different way.

She even shared with me, "I am so glad I can give myself permission every day to not be afraid to think about Ra. Now that I understand that my feelings are normal, I am able to reflect on the times Ra and I spent on the bed snuggling. This memory now fills my heart with joy."

Stage Five: Adjustment to Life

Once Melissa began to understand the stages of grief, she began to experience her life in a different way. She started to allow herself to feel happy, and she even began to explore the idea of adopting another cat (more on this point in chapter 10).

She confided one day, "Wendy, I have felt so many crazy and uncomfortable things during the past year. Oh my goodness, it is hard to believe that I can actually think of Ra now and have joy back in my heart when I think of him. I am now ready to move on, but I don't want to disrespect my bond with Ra. How do I do that?"

This was a great place for Melissa to be in her grief journey, and she poses a question that most of my clients also ask. Throughout this book, we will be talking about adjusting to a new life in more detail. Yet for now, keep in mind that this period is about integrating these changes into your daily life to help you rescue your joy and not forget or disrespect your cat.

I have recorded a Healing Cat Loss Meditation to help you navigate through your emotions, decisions, and healing while on the pet loss journey. You can download your free mp3 by going to the beginning of this book.

This meditation will help you adjust to your new life too.

Stage Six: Your New Normal

As Melissa adjusted to her life and the changes of not having Ra present, she began to not be concerned about what other people thought of her grief. Also she began to look for another cat. She adjusted to the myriad changes in her new life and recognized that her heart was ready to open to another cat. She knew that by getting another cat, she wasn't being disrespectful to Ra and that Ra still held a very special place in her soul.

Melissa started to work at her local humane society as a volunteer in a special program that helped cats that were difficult to place for adoption. She loved her new volunteer position and six months later adopted a cat that she was able to help.

Stage Seven: Acceptance and Hope

When Melissa began to experience the last stage of pet grief, she was ready to move forward with an entirely different attitude. She accepted the fact that Ra had died.

Melissa found her new normal and had a plan of action on how she was going to share her life with her new cat—the food, the doctors, the new activities. Now she could live every day with joy, hope, and a desire to do the best she could with her new cat.

This was the stage when she became more aware and accepted her grief stages. She was confident that she could provide everything that her new cat needed. It was easier to make decisions through whatever stage of grief she was experiencing.

Did Melissa forget Ra at this stage? No, she did not! She was able to recognize that death is something that we cannot avoid. And that death does allow for new life and love.

Chapter Wrap-Up

These stages are references to guide you on how you can process your particular pet loss grief. Melissa experienced all the stages. By no means do you need to experience them all as Melissa did or even move through the stages in the given order.

Use the three *Contemplation Questions* at the end of this chapter to help guide you through your unique stages of grief.

Again, please remember that you are not alone in your grief journey. There are others that are experiencing the same thing as you.

In the next chapter, I am going to teach you about the myths that surround pet grief and how these myths can hold you back from healing your grief. I am also going to show you how you can turn these myths around so that they can help you with your journey.

Chapter 2 Contemplation Questions

1. What are the stages of grief that you have experienced? Are you experiencing them in the presented sequence?

2. What have you learned about your unique journey through each of these stages? How is it helpful to know what stages you are experiencing?

3. Wendy helps her clients know and understand the seven stages of pet grief early in their journeys. Her clients find that by knowing this valuable information early on, rather than later, they are better prepared for the future. In what ways do you predict that knowing this information now will help you better prepare for the future?

3. Discerning the Pet Loss Myths

Now that you have an understanding of what constitutes normal grief (chapter 1) and have explored the seven stages of grief (chapter 2), we are going to visit the multitude of myths that come along with pet grief after your cat dies.

It is important to consider these myths on your healing journey. We have many pre-conceived ideas as to what death is about and how we "should" react to it or dread it. No matter where you are with your beliefs, it is important to approach these myths with an openness and willingness to heal.

To introduce the myths, let's explore the experience of Sandi, a client whom I supported in her grief journey after the loss of her beloved calico, Foxtail.

Myth Confrontation: Sandi and Foxtail

My client Sandi, on our third call, was destroyed when her co-worker said to her one day, "How can you still be sad about your cat? Cats don't care about people, they are so independent. It's not like Foxtail was waiting by the door for you when you got home from work each day. You can get a better cat. I'll help you pick one out."

Initially in sharing this story, Sandi was beyond shocked and hurt. "How could my co-worker say this to me? She knew I was in pain." Sandi started to question herself and was even thinking that her co-worker was right. Then suddenly, as she was explaining this to me, she started to laugh. She was horrified that she had been laughing, which made her begin to cry. She told me that when she thought of this conversation, it oftentimes made her feel so sad, which then, strangely to her, led to a laughing spell! She felt horrible and confused about the laughter. She felt disrespectful to Foxtail.

My response—"Sandi, that's just a grief myth. Don't you believe it. You are going to live out a variety of emotions, and laughter is just one that you are going to experience on your grief journey."

With my guidance, Sandi permitted herself to have a range of feelings, including laughter, and she continued to understand how unhealthy it was to disrespect her emotions. She allowed the laughter and the tears to come. In doing so, she felt relief. She was able to breathe and understand that laughing was another way to express her grief. She felt as if a heavy weight had been lifted from her heart.

In debunking the "no joy during grieving" myth, Sandi finished her session feeling a lot stronger on her journey. She had renewed confidence that she could heal her pain with more clarity and understanding.

Myths about grieving, like the one Sandi voiced, have been around for a long time, and they can either really help you with your grief or be a hindrance to your healing process. The key to making these myths help you is to be aware of them, know how you feel about them, and then debunk them.

The Myths

1. *It is selfish and extravagant to mourn and grieve the death of a cat when our world has so much human suffering.*

Debunking—You are a cat-lover, and you understand how important your cat was to you. The grief surrounding the fact that your cherished cat died is significant and important to you.

People are capable of simultaneously grieving both animals and humans. One doesn't detract from the other. Grief, as well as love, isn't "either/or"; it is "both/and." By grieving and mourning your cat, you are showing tremendous compassion for the world at large. That is a wonderful trait to have. Realizing that your heart is capable of such love will give you a tremendous amount of strength to heal—and to love again, both animals and people.

2. *I must follow the seven stages of grief in their exact order so that I can truly heal my pain.*

Debunking—Grief is not about following a prescribed list. Grief is tenacious and can really dig into your heart, which can affect your daily routine and then render you hopeless.

The last thing that you need to be worried about is following the seven stages of grief in a precise order. Although the stages of grief are extremely valuable, the order in which you experience them is up to you. Let the stages unfold naturally.

3. *There is a right and wrong way to grieve.*

Debunking—As with following the seven stages of grief in chronological order, the same is true about your unique grief experience—meaning there is not a single correct experience.

Your relationship with your cat was special. No two people grieve the same way. While one person may feel sadness, another person may feel anger about their cat dying. Your grief journey is yours and very unique—stick with that!

Grieving is very personal and individual to your experiences with your cat. It depends on your personality, the personality of your cat, the nature of their illness (if they had one) or death, and your coping style.

4. *The best thing to do is to grieve and mourn alone, especially because it is just a cat.*

Debunking—We have been taught that in order to be strong and independent we should not share our grief. It would burden others, and it is inappropriate to let other people know how we are feeling.

That simply isn't true. In fact, it is important to reach out to others who will honestly support you and not judge your process. You will want to protect yourself from being judged for loving, grieving, and mourning the death of your cat, so it is important that you select carefully the people whom you reach out to. Your experience of loss and grief is a tender time to be fully cherished by you and in the way you decide.

Take your time choosing whom you turn to for support because some people don't understand or take pet loss seriously. Find a support group, pet loss coach, and/or friend that will allow you to talk about your grief without making you feel crazy or weird. We address this more in chapter 6.

Also, remember, if there ever comes a time when you can no longer function in life, please see the appropriate healthcare provider.

5. *I have to be "strong" in my grief.*

Debunking—In general our society teaches that grief feelings can be a sign of weakness, especially in regard to animals.

Feeling sad, frightened, lonely, or depressed are all normal reactions. Crying doesn't mean that you are weak. In fact, it takes strength to accept and engage with these difficult emotions and to cry.

Let yourself feel those emotions, physical sensations, and spiritual challenges that you are going through. There is a reason you are having these feelings. Plus, there is no reason why you need to feel that you have to "protect" your family or friends by being (supposedly) strong.

Showing your feelings will help you and may even help them. By showing your feelings, you are also debunking the first myth about pet loss grief being selfish. When you show your feelings, you are saying, "I have compassion for living beings." And that, my friend, is extremely beautiful!

6. *Grief will go away someday.*

Debunking—Never! And that is okay. Our grief changes as each day goes by. You will never forget your cat, yet your feelings of grief will change, and there will be a time when you will feel joy again.

Never feel like you have to rush through your grief journey. It takes time. Patience and not judging yourself come in handy when you are experiencing the stages of grief.

Your goal for healing your pet loss is not to "get over it." We never stop feeling grief for losing a pet. But we learn to move forward in life again with fond memories.

7. *No one gets my pet grief, and I am alone in what I am experiencing.*

Debunking—You are never alone with the grief that you are going through. It may feel like that at times because some people don't know what it feels like to lose the companionship of their cat. They just don't understand what you are going through.

People (even cat-lovers) will say unsupportive things, like "There are so many cats that need homes. See this as an opportunity!" or "At least it wasn't a child." Even still, there are many, many people who do know the grief you are experiencing. It just may take some time to find the right people to support you in a healthy way. There are supportive friends, end-of-life and grief coaches, and pet loss support groups to walk the journey with you. We will talk about this more in chapter 6.

Remember—you are not alone with your pet loss grief.

8. *Pet loss grief will go away.*

Debunking—Many of my clients call me when they have just gotten the news that their cats died. Some even call me years later. They feel a tremendous amount of grief and just want it to go away.

It takes work to heal pet loss grief. Feel comfortable and take your time. Be an active participant so that you can experience the stages of grief.

Your cat was really special to you. It is really important to let your emotions happen and to experience them. If you feel like the feelings will go away on their own, you are only stuffing them in. The grief will still change, but it may take longer, and you may not learn the powerful lessons of grief.

And as many of my clients say, "Grief has a great talent of surprising you when you least expect it." So it is better to actively acknowledge, process, and experience it than to stuff it down only for it to pop up at surprising times and in unwelcoming forms.

9. *Once I do all the grief work, it will go away.*

Debunking—Once you do all the work in your grieving process, remember that grief can come up again. It is not uncommon to have deep feelings of grief appear again, even years later. It is normal for this to happen.

Grief never goes away, and that is okay. Many of my clients report that when their grief shows up after a few months or years, they are happy about it because it gives them a chance to say, "I love you," to their cats again.

For now, if you just lost your cat or are just beginning to work on your grief, tuck this thought in a special place, so you know what to expect later.

10. *Having a feeling of joy at moments in my life soon after my cat has died is not good.*

Debunking—Here is the thing—your companion has died. Your cat was maybe very sick, elderly, or suffered a traumatic death.

The last thing that you probably think you are allowed to feel is joyful or happy. In fact, you probably are feeling many emotions from this news. All your emotions are valid and okay to feel.

It is okay to experience moments of joy, even when you are grieving about your cat's death. It is healthy and doesn't mean you are forgetting your cat's situation or disrespecting your cat.

Joy and laughter are normal responses. This is your body giving you a breather from the stress, pain, anxiety, etc. It is a survival mechanism that you do not need to fear. Joy is first aid for the soul.

11. *It is horrible to feel happy or relieved that my cat died.*

Debunking—If you had a cat that was suffering, there may be a little place in your mind that felt relief once they died.

If this is so, when the time has come and your cat has reached the end of their life, you may feel relieved and even slightly glad. This is a very common feeling for my clients that suffered the pain and angst of losing their cats to terminal illnesses.

When your cat is in pain and suffering every day, it can take a lot out of you, emotionally, physically, and spiritually. It breaks your heart and can leave you feeling hopeless and helpless. At your cat's death, feeling slightly glad and even relieved are also very normal feelings of grief. Keep in mind that these are not due to selfishness, but simply relief that your cat is no longer suffering in the physical world.

The Other Side of the Myths: Grace and Compassion

These myths are very common, and many people think they are true. These myths, in conjunction with the inappropriate comments that people make (more on these in chapter 4), can easily trigger your grief. If you are not aware of the myths, you may become confused as to why suddenly you are feeling sad or very angry.

Even though they may be well-meaning friends, family, or co-workers, when one of them offers you a myth as a so-called "word of wisdom," it can pack a powerful punch to trigger your pet loss grief. However, once you become aware of these myths and why they are not true, you will be able to react to them with grace and compassion for yourself and your beloved companion.

Here is the thing about believing these myths and letting them affect you—I have seen in my practice that when folks believe and live by these myths, they get stuck in their grief and have a difficult time gaining personal peace.

When they learn to take these myths, debunk them, and replace them with positive thoughts and actions, they are able to spend more time loving their cats that have died, rather than being stressed-out with unknown anxiety or other feelings of grief that they may be experiencing.

Please revisit these myths and the debunking of them. They will help you be prepared for the multitude of thoughts and feelings that you will have and the comments people will make.

Use the chapter's three *Contemplation Questions* to help you to identify and then debunk any myths that you may encounter on your journey.

Chapter Wrap-Up

Myths about pet loss grief can be roadblocks to moving forward with meaning and purpose in regard to the bond you have with your cherished cat.

The way to remove the roadblocks and make the myths work for you is to be aware of them, debunk them, and then replace them with something positive.

To repeat, always remember—you are not alone in your grief journey. There are others that are experiencing the same thing as you. Find those people and spend time with them.

In chapter 4, I am going to help you prepare for the insensitive things that people will say to you and how these statements can trigger your grief unexpectedly. I am also going to show you how to be aware of these statements before they happen, so you can prepare yourself and won't be totally thrown if you encounter them.

Chapter 3 Contemplation Questions

1. Since your cat is no longer physically with you, have you experienced any myths given in this chapter? If so, reflect on that experience.

2. Now that you have encountered several of the common myths surrounding pet loss grief, add other myths that you may be experiencing. Can you debunk them and pull something positive out of them?

3. Notice which myths you relate to. Write them down and then rewrite them in a positive way. Post them in a prominent place so that frequently you can be reminded what is really true.

4. Managing Inappropriate Comments

When a family member, co-worker, stranger you meet at the store, or even your best friend tries to reassure you by commenting, "I can't believe you are still talking about your cat . . . What was its name anyway? . . . Time to get over it—don't you think?" you may immediately feel surprised and hurt, thinking, "What did I just hear and how do I react?"

You may find that you start to feel different sensations in your body, and you may even feel a little off-center physically. Quite abruptly, you may feel enormously sad. Like your well-being totally changed. You may start to feel uncomfortable, yet you don't know what to do. Should you just smile and say, "Thank you," or should you politely turn away and go about your business?

The first thing to come to terms with is that people are going to say hurtful things like this to you. People want to be helpful, so they'll say these things that they think are helpful and well-meaning. However, in reality their words about your beloved companion's death are totally off the mark and very unsupportive, so much so that they can trigger an unexpected feeling or reaction. I will warn you, most of the time you will feel unprepared for these unsupportive statements.

What is happening when people say these unintentionally unsupportive things is that they are inadvertently fueling and activating your grief. You become sad, depressed, angry, or confused, and you are not sure why, all of a sudden, you are feeling this way. You likely become confused as to how to handle these people and even wonder if you should continue being friends.

Let me repeat—it is normal for people to say unsupportive, yet what they think are well-meaning, things to someone who has lost a cat. And it is also customary for you to have the uncomfortable and confusing reactions that you are having.

Now here is the thing—as a society we have gotten very distant from the dying process. We view it as something to be afraid of, and we may even want to avoid it. As people, the more we accept death and allow our grief to happen in a safe environment, then the healthier this process will be.

Remember—your confused and heightened reaction to the person's statement is common, and it is important to not believe or internalize what they have said.

I am going to teach you in this chapter how you can use what you've learned about grief itself (from chapter 1) and the stages of grief (from chapter 2), so you can handle the situation with compassion, respect, and grace.

Case Study—Jannie and White Paws

Jannie, whose cat White Paws died from throat cancer, told me during one of her sessions that after she'd told her cousin about her experience of losing White Paws, her cousin started to make excuses about being too busy to meet for coffee.

Jannie felt very sad about this because she liked her cousin and she knew her cousin was avoiding her. Jannie explained, "My cat just died, my cousin and I are very close, and she never made excuses before. Now she is avoiding me and has said some really hurtful things."

You can expect this to happen to you. Because, as with Jannie's experience, people fear and like to avoid the topic of death, so some will evade dealing with it—no matter what. As a society we aren't versed in how to go about supporting each other in a healthy way when someone is experiencing grief of any kind.

When Jannie became aware of the unsupportive things her cousin and others were saying, she prepared herself on how she was going to react. The beautiful result of this was she found that her support team suddenly grew and she had new friends that truly understood and supported her.

Your Reaction

Right now I want to share how you can be prepared for the hurtful things that people will say to you.

I promise you are going to hear them every day, not from everyone, but you will hear them from people that you thought understood what you are going through—just like what happened with Jannie.

This is a huge part of your journey when dealing with your cat's death. Be ready, be prepared, and take control of these situations, so you know that what you are feeling is okay and normal.

Here are a few of the many things people typically say that my clients have experienced. (At the end of this chapter, you will have the opportunity to list some of your own.)

Hurtful Things That People Say

1. *It's only a cat . . . You can get another.*

As a cat parent, you know that the relationship that you had with your dear cat was unique to the both of you. No one else had the relationship that you two did.

When someone says to you, "It's only a cat and you can get another," this is the time for you to respond, "Thank you," and make your exit. To engage and try to educate this person only takes time and can be extremely exhausting. It is your sole job when experiencing grief to not exert your emotional and physical energies on those that do not understand.

2. *I am so sorry to hear that.*

This one is a big one and the most popular thing to say when we get the news that someone's cat died. The fact is that it is not that person's fault that your cat reached the end of their life.

I know it may be a moot point, but a kinder, more supportive, and compassionate way to respond to this type of news is "I am so sad to hear that your cat died. Would you like me to listen to what you are feeling?" This type of comment will give you a safe place to express your grief rather than feeling like you have to take care of the other person's sadness or have to protect yourself from feeling even more grief.

The way you can react to the "I am sorry" response is NOT to thank them. Because, remember, it is not your job to take care of someone else. Silence, a small smile, followed by a gentle head nod is all that is needed. If they persist, you can politely excuse yourself.

3. *You are still grieving?*

"You are still grieving?" is a very insensitive question to pose to someone that is feeling sad or depressed that their cat died. It suggests that there should be a time limit on the grief process and that you've taken it too far.

Prepare yourself by falling back on what you've learned about grief thus far in the book—grieving doesn't just go away, and it does not have a timetable. Remember, take as much time as is necessary with your grieving.

This question oftentimes helps people know who their real support team is. If you hear this question, you can politely respond, "Yes, I am," and then make your exit. You really don't want to waste your time with people that just don't get it.

4. *Let me tell you what I did after my cat died . . .*

This is another tough one. Although it may seem supportive, it can also be overwhelming and create feelings of guilt. Your cat may have just died or you are six months into your grief journey. You may be trying to figure out where all the pieces of the puzzle go in your new situation. Opening yourself up to a ton of advice at this time could be helpful, but it could also increase your feelings of anxiety, guilt, hopelessness, and being overwhelmed.

You can pick and choose what advice you want to listen to. We will explore this in more detail later in this book by offering ways for you to make decisions based on your own terms, beliefs, and experiences.

However, right now, a good way to respond to this fourth comment is "I appreciate your thoughts of concern, but I really just need to process my feelings at this time."

Please use the three *Contemplation Questions* at the end of this chapter to guide you to become aware of and prepare your reaction to these kinds of statements.

Your Support Team

You are the expert when it comes to your grief journey after your cat is no longer physically in your life. Your grief journey is unique, and no two people deal the same way with losing a cat to a life-threatening illness, age, or traumatic accident.

The important thing to remember is to choose the people that you interact with wisely during this special time. Choose those that truly support you, listen, don't judge you, and only give you advice when you ask them.

That type of support is available to you. You don't need to feel alone and go through this journey without support and compassion.

When you find these people, consider them friends to help you never have to walk the journey of pet loss grief alone again. In chapter 6, we will talk about ways in which you can get support.

Chapter Wrap-Up

This chapter is aimed at helping you become aware of the unsupportive things that people are going to say to you while you are coping with pet loss. This is common—and it is also understandable that their words will trigger grief in you.

The key to responding to such statements with compassion and grace is to prepare yourself and to entrench yourself in the truth about grief (chapter 1) and its seven stages (chapter 2). You will use this chapter's *Contemplation Questions* to help you to become aware of and prepare your reaction to these statements.

Also, you may want to actively find one, two, or more people who will serve as your "support team," listening to you and allowing you to live out your grief as it naturally happens.

In chapter 5, I am going to share with you ways that our society puts high demands on our emotions and how we process them. It is not considered a positive thing when we take time out of our fast-paced lives to mourn our losses. Instead, we are encouraged to get over them fast and not take the appropriate time to heal. You will gain an understanding on how to break through those demands so that you are able to grieve and pay tribute to your memories.

Chapter 4 Contemplation Questions

1. Which "Hurtful Things That People Say" comments have you heard? Have you received other comments that triggered your grief? If so, write them down.

2. How did you respond to the statements that you listed above, and how did you support yourself and/or take control of the situation?

3. List the names of the people that you are comfortable with and how they are supporting you. Do you seek them out on a daily, weekly, or monthly basis?

5. Understanding the Future

After your cat dies, many changes are going to happen to you besides your personal grief journey. Your life is going to change and things are going to be different now that your companion is no longer with you.

You are going to be faced with needing to make some important decisions about burial, cremation, or when it is appropriate to get another cat. You are also going to be challenged to be mindful of your own health as you navigate your changed life.

As mentioned already, it is essential and important to take all the time that you need for your grieving and then to know what to expect during this process in order to heal your pet loss.

We live in a society that has high demands on our emotions and how we process them. It is not considered a positive act when we take time out of our fast-paced lives to experience and mourn our losses. Instead, we are encouraged to get over them fast and not take the appropriate time to heal.

Because of societal norms, we often become impatient with our grieving and healing, and have forgotten that quality takes time. When your cat dies and you are experiencing grief, it just cannot be rushed and expected of you to get on with your life.

As you learned in chapters 1 and 2, grief is normal and has a life of its own, and it is perfectly common to feel the way you do. From the myths and unsupportive comments others may make, you also learned that grief is feared by our society.

Since our society is very fast-paced, we are expected to move through our feelings without much notice and get back to being productive right away. We are rushed to return to work and encouraged to stop crying and to get over loss in lightning-speed time. There's an entire list of additional expectations that can be nearly impossible when facing grief.

Yet, wouldn't it be wonderful if we would slow down and allow our emotions to heal on their own terms?

Case Study — Maggie and Fred

My client Maggie had a cat named Fred who wandered off one day. She searched for him daily but couldn't find him. Then one week after his disappearance she was running in the park and found some of his fur. The feelings of grief that Maggie expressed were heart-wrenching and traumatic.

When Maggie first called me, she was extremely horrified and was feeling so guilty that Fred had escaped (he wasn't an outdoor cat). She didn't know what to do with her overwhelming feelings of grief. She divulged, "I can't believe I was so irresponsible and left the door unlocked. I was in such a hurry to get to an appointment that I forgot to make sure the latch was closed. I will never get over this feeling of grief, remorse, and pain—but I want to—and fast."

During our sessions, I helped Maggie realize that her situation could not be rushed. Feeling and expecting to get over it quickly was not a healthy way of dealing with her grief. Her life with Fred was very special, and to expect that she rush herself was an unfair expectation.

Instead, I encouraged Maggie to face her grief and emotions—to engage with them. And if she did the work that it takes to be present in her stages of grief and mourning, her grief experience would become less raw. In my practice, I encourage clients to take the time that they need to heal.

While there is no timetable for getting over grief, as you already learned in chapter 2, there are different stages in the grief journey. Some are more difficult than others, and that difficulty is unique to the relationship that you had with your cat.

However, just like the different stages, keep in mind in the days, weeks, months, and even years after your loss that time will be one of your greatest healers and is on your side a hundred percent. Even though you may feel that you cannot survive another day because the grief is so overwhelming, you can and you will.

The First Days and Weeks After

Here is what you may experience during the first few days and weeks after your cat dies:

- My clients often feel numb during the first few days and weeks. There are so many changes during this time, and it takes some getting used to when you suddenly do not have to take care of your buddy and your home is more silent and much less active. Life becomes a blur.

- It can also be draining and painful. Your grief demands attention, and the newness of your loss starts to settle in.

- The void that you are probably feeling is beyond huge, and there is absolutely nothing that you can do to fill such emptiness. This numbness is part of normal grief that we talked about in chapter 1, yet you might be feeling other emotions as well.

- One of these is denial, which is huge and very common during this time. You may be feeling that it was a bad dream or some mistake or maybe your cat is just outside, enjoying the sunshine, and will be coming in shortly for dinner.

- This denial can even be stronger if their death was sudden or accidental. Many times it lasts longer than it does when you lose a cat to illness or old age.

- Anger and intense frustration are common emotions during this early time period and can easily continue for years.

My client Maggie was deeply irritated and upset with herself that she didn't check the door before she left her home. If she had, then Fred would still be alive. She was aggravated at herself also because she hadn't been able to find Fred before he died.

One of the best things that you can do during this time is "nothing." Seriously. You do not need to clean the house, rake the lawn, do errands, or go to the movies with friends if you do not want to. However, if any of these activities will help you feel better, then by all means, do them.

It is truly not the time to go deep with trying to process your grief.

It is often very helpful to relax and give yourself permission to feel your loss. It is also a time to be sure that you are eating healthy and doing something that is nurturing for yourself, like spending time in nature or getting a massage (more in chapter 6).

Three Months After

It takes about three months for your grief to intensify, and in my experience, the three-month time period is extremely painful and challenging.

Your shock, denial, and disbelief are starting to wear off, and you are beginning to understand the reality of the death of your beloved companion.

It can also be a time when your friends, family, and co-workers have moved on, themselves, so they are encouraging you now to move on too. This can add to the intensity of grief because you may start wondering what is wrong with you.

Having a pet loss grief coach or pet loss support team can be really important for you at this time because they will provide you with the needed support and care by giving you a calm place to express your grief and mourn. They will listen to your story without judgment or impatience.

First Anniversary of the Death

I never had a client that forgot the anniversary of the first year of their cat's death. Because it marks such a painful time in the history of the life that you spent together, how could you not feel intense grief?

The pain of your grief will be just as intense as it was when you experienced your initial feelings of loss. Also, be aware that your anticipation of the anniversary date can be as painful, if not worse than, the anniversary itself.

Twenty Years Later — Tara and Puddles

Read what Tara shares about her childhood cat named Puddles, twenty years later:

Puddles, it has been twenty years since we shared our lives together. I have gone through so much, and I miss you every day. I hope you know I love you still with all of my heart, and I thank you for all the lessons that you taught me. So today, the anniversary of your death, I celebrate all the wonderful moments I had with you. Thank you for being in my life.

It is important for you to have support and be able to talk through and plan how you want to spend the anniversary, which we will talk about in chapter 12.

Keep in mind that this is part of your healing process. You may want to honor your cat with a special celebration recounting your prized memories.

This first anniversary can bring new awareness to your healing journey and bring to the surface opportunities to move forward with your process.

Holidays, Birthdays & Special Days

Just like the first anniversary—holidays, birthdays, and special days that you spent with your loved cat can be excruciating and devastating to experience and/or remember.

For instance, holidays when you are supposed to be happy but you aren't can be super tough to navigate. When you observe everyone around you, smiling and celebrating, yet your heart is breaking, it can easily make you feel very alone with your loss.

If you are feeling this during a holiday celebration, the last thing you want to do is join in the merriment. It is okay if you don't. One of the most helpful tools that I share with my clients is to take a break.

The bathroom is the perfect place. If you feel as if you are going to cry, feel sad, or have anxiety or any other feelings of grief, you can go to the bathroom, shut the door, and have a moment to collect your thoughts and feelings before returning to a room full of people.

Maggie did this a lot. It was a way for her to feel safe, take a breath, and remember Fred in peace. It was her special way to deal with holidays with a family that expected her to move quickly through her grief.

Birthdays are another tough time as are the anniversaries that you had with your cat. They act as triggers for your grief. They are reminders of your loss. Yet, they can be excellent opportunities for helping you move to the next step of your journey, so you can make new choices and discover new ways of navigating your life.

There are many helpful ways to survive these days by paying tribute to your cat, which we will cover in chapters 12, 13, and 15, with specific suggestions on how to create memorials and markers of time that demonstrate your respect and caring for your cat.

Chapter Wrap-Up

In this chapter, we covered what to expect days, weeks, and years after the death of your beloved companion. By understanding the demands that our society places on our emotions and how we process them, you are reminded and encouraged to take the time you need to heal.

With the *Contemplation Questions* at the end of this chapter, you will take control of the time you need to experience your grief, and you will be ready to not be influenced by those around you to move faster.

In chapter 6, I am going to share ways for you to take care of yourself. I am going to give you reasons and examples of ways in which you can restore and support yourself during this painful and raw time.

Chapter 5 Contemplation Questions

1. In what ways are you feeling rushed with your grief journey? Who is rushing you?

2. What are you going to do to not rush your experience, to slow down and be where you are? What are the ways you can be prepared if someone tries to rush you?

3. How have you spent, or are going to spend, the first anniversary of your cat's end of life? Write down the feelings of grief you are experiencing. If your cat has not been physically with you for years, how have you spent the anniversaries?

6. Caring for Your Soul

You now know that grief is a persuasive force that has many personalities that can affect your well-being. When your cat is no longer with you every day, your normal existence is altered. This experience changes and affects your life in many ways. It can literally disturb your daily routine and steal your vitality.

However, allowing time for self-care in order to survive your loss is extremely helpful and important. Grief has a tendency to thrive when we are tired and at a loss. When we are rested, our chaotic minds are unable to overcome our senses.

While most of my clients feel guilty for resting and taking care of themselves during the period of initial loss, everyone needs downtime to heal and refresh. It is totally okay to do this. Not only is it okay, it is necessary. Self-care is actually a great way to manage your pet grief journey and allow greater focus, strength, and compassion to shine through.

Remember the free meditation that you downloaded at the beginning of this book? This meditation was created so that you can take a relaxing break to rejuvenate your soul. Please refer back to it to help you take care of yourself.

Case Study—Ellen and Twinkles

After Twinkles died, Ellen was unable to relax. She ate standing up and couldn't sit down—even for a moment. This was difficult for her because her job required sitting at a desk. She found herself standing most of the time, which made her co-workers uncomfortable and they started to complain. Ellen told me, "Every time I sit down, I start to think about Twinkles."

What happened? Ellen stopped taking care of herself by avoiding her grief. If she sat down, she would be reminded of what she was feeling.

When Ellen reached out to me and we started to work together, we set up a self-care plan that she was comfortable with. As the weeks went by, Ellen stuck to the plan and experienced some wonderful changes.

She found that as she became healthier, her grief was less intense and she was able to reflect on her memories with Twinkles without feeling miserable. Plus, she was finally able to sit down to eat a healthy meal and not work standing up. She also was able to make some tough decisions that she'd had been avoiding, which we will talk about more in the next section of this book.

The Best Advice

Now please listen closely to the best advice that I can give you right now and that I gave to Ellen—take some time for self-care right away. You may have been experiencing grief for a while or your grief may be new. It doesn't matter where you are in the grief journey; what matters is that you replenish your own body, mind, and soul.

The connection and your memories that you have with your cat will not go away if you take time to feel better. In fact, it will make your memories stronger and will help you heal during this terrible and devastating time.

If you are tired, burned-out, stressed-out, not eating, and not sleeping because your grief is so strong and you are feeling so incredibly alone, it will be difficult for you to make some important decisions. The last thing you want to do is make a decision that you will later regret.

Like Ellen, this is the time to take care of yourself so that you are functioning at the best you can and not relying on your reserves to get you through. Having strength is critical for you to be ready for any unexpected feelings of grief and for proceeding with your new life.

The "What" of Self-Care

There are many things that you can do for yourself that don't cost a lot of money: walking in nature, taking a nap, taking a bath, hanging out with friends, listening to relaxing music, or having a cup of tea.

Create a self-care plan that you would love to experience and that will give you the greatest support. Creating a successful self-care plan that includes some new activities as well as old activities that have already given you joy will ground you during this difficult time.

Remember, the healthier you are in body, mind, and spirit, the easier it is to cope and deal with the grief that you are going through. This is a tough period of loss no matter where you are in regard to the timeframe. Giving yourself some downtime will ease some of the pain and heal your grief as you continue your journey.

The Physical Self

Let's talk about some of the options for taking care of your physical body during this time. This is the time to put your grief on the shelf and just focus on you.

Your grief will have its chance to come back and challenge you, but for right now, this time is about you.

My clients find that when they do one or more of the following physical things for their bodies, they feel stronger and more in control of their grief. Even if they can do one of these things for only five to ten minutes a day, it still helps them on their journeys.

I suggest that you spend at least a half-hour every day if you can with any combination of the following activities for the health of your body, mind, and spirit:

- Massage

- Walks in nature

- Reiki or other forms of energy work

- Exercise class

- Nutritious and regular eating

- Plentiful sleep

- Short breaks throughout the day with your eyes closed

- Intentional and active breathing

If a half-hour every day is too much time, try to give yourself at least a half-hour three times a week during which you take care of your physical body.

The Mental Self

The next thing to take care of is your mind. As you know, your mind is going in a million different directions right now. Sometimes your mind clutter is creating so much anxiety and stress you wonder how you're going to manage.

To help your mind, you can find support groups, pet loss grief coaches, psychotherapists, friends, co-workers, family members, and veterinarians who respect the journey of pet grief you are going through. They should be there for you and be able to walk this journey with you so that you don't have to feel alone.

Finding ways to support your mind's health can take some time, yet if you know what you're looking for, the process can be less cumbersome.

Here are some other ways that you can create a healthy mind that can support you:

- Talk to a pet grief coach—a coach will listen and allow you to better manage your healing process.

- Talk to a psychotherapist or other healthcare provider—it is important to find someone that gets pet loss.

- Participate in pet loss support groups—these provide another way to support you. In them you will meet people that are going through similar situations. Be sure you find one where you feel that you are getting ample time to express your journey and are not being judged by anyone.

- Talk with select family and friends—this is a tough one. Your friends and family may mean well, yet they may also be the ones that trigger your grief because they really don't know how to support you. Choose wisely and choose only those friends and family that let you talk and that don't offer advice. Definitely stay away from the ones that judge you!

A healthy mind is a strong mind that creates balance when the mind clutter starts getting out of hand. Having a support system helps you monitor your mind and offers solutions when your grief is swirling out of control.

Choose a couple of these options that feel good to you. Do some research and don't feel bad if the person that you thought was your best friend doesn't support you. There is someone who will!

The Spiritual Self

Now let's talk about your spiritual health. Many times you can forget about this one when experiencing the newness of the death of your cat. You may even be uncomfortable with your spiritual beliefs or not have any.

Whatever your spiritual choice, remember, it is your journey. I encourage you to only incorporate a spiritual practice into your daily life if you feel comfortable doing so.

Here are some of the ways that you can create spiritual health in your life:

- Meditation comes in all forms. A quiet walk in the woods is equally meditative as sitting quietly in one posture and clearing your mind of all thoughts.

- Yoga, tai chi, or other forms of spiritual-physical practice help your body become stronger. The discipline and focus create a connection to your inner spiritual force.

- Your spiritual practice, no matter what your belief is, and its daily, weekly, or periodic expression can help you receive solace.

- An animal medium or animal communicator is an excellent way to get peace of mind and explore the spiritual connection that you have with your cat, even after their death, from your cat's perspective. My clients that choose to have an animal mediumship session with me are greatly relieved to hear from their cats again (more on this in chapter 15).

I have shared with you many ways to take care of yourself. It is totally up to you on how you would like to include one or many of the suggestions that I offered.

Remember, this is a trying time, and it can become very difficult as the days, weeks, and months progress. You are dealing with a huge shift in your daily life. Your dear pal is no longer physically present, and that is a lot to handle.

Creating a support team as we discussed is equally important as taking care of yourself. Being well rested, balanced, at peace are all the things you need to meet your grief head-on!

Use the *Contemplation Questions* at the end of the chapter to take action on your own self-care without guilt. Even if the only thing you can do right now is simple breathing to create balance in your life, that is okay!

Chapter Wrap-Up

In this chapter, I shared ways that helped so many of my clients find peace of mind and strength after their cats died. I encourage you to take some time for yourself without feeling guilty. Care for yourself in terms of your body, mind, and spirit.

By allowing time in your schedule for self-care, you will be able to move through your grief journey with more quality and awareness. You will make better decisions and be ready for unexpected grief too.

Remember to use the three *Contemplation Questions* to determine the what, when, and how of your own self-care.

In section 2, I am going to offer you support with the extremely difficult and sometimes painful decisions that you will be faced with and that need to be addressed.

Chapter 6 Contemplation Questions

1. How much time can you carve out for rejuvenating your soul—daily, weekly, and monthly?

2. How are you going to reach out to get support for your body and mind?

3. How are you going to support your spiritual beliefs? How are you going to practice your spiritual beliefs, so they directly support you with your emotions and stages of grief?

DECISIONS TO BE MADE: SECTION TWO

How lucky I am to have something that makes saying good-bye so hard.

—A.A. Milne

7. Tending to Your Cat's Body

One thing that we can all depend on in life is death. Death happens to everyone, and we can't avoid it. By knowing and embracing your beliefs about hospice, the end of life, and the afterlife, your decision on how to care for your cat's body will inspire you to feel absolute about the life that you had with your cat.

We can look at death as a valuable teaching experience in terms of how we relate to the cycle of life and our beliefs. Death deserves attention and respect. Your decisions about what to do with the body of your dear companion will give you the sense that you valued and appreciated the life you had with your cat.

Remember that how you choose to care for your cat's body is your way of showing respect for yourself and the relationship you had with another living being. If you show love for your cat by choosing cremation, burial in your backyard, or burial in a pet cemetery (chapter 8) instead of letting your veterinarian take care of everything—that is absolutely okay. No one's judgment of you matters because it is you and your relationship with your cat that is the most important consideration.

I'm going to let you in on a little secret here—when you actively participate in deciding how to care for your cat's body, that nagging and painful grief feeling of guilt doesn't have much chance of surviving. Instead, by choosing how you are going to handle the body, making decisions, and taking an active role, you are going to win, and guilt will not have a chance.

I find in my practice mostly everybody, including myself, feels some level of guilt that we never did enough for our treasured cats. Know that this sentiment is common and universal.

Yet, when you take control, deciding how you are going to care for your cat's body in the most suitable way and how you will pay tribute to your cat, which we will cover in chapters 12 and 13, guilt cannot live in your heart. The only thing that continues to live in your heart is the love that you shared with your valued feline companion and the fact that you did the right thing.

Making sure that the body of your feline companion is handled perfectly is not strange or peculiar. It shows courage, pride, and strength, all of which are incredibly powerful when you are experiencing such great loss and grief.

The Pros and Cons

There are a few things to consider that can help you decide how to handle your cat's body.

When your veterinarian confronts you, asking, "What would you like to do with the body?" there are a couple of options for you to consider:

1. You can leave your cat with your veterinarian to take care of everything.

2. You can take your cat home to be buried or to a crematorium.

Either way or whatever your choice, there are pros and cons.

Option One: *You can leave your cat with your veterinarian to take care of everything.*

Option One Pros

If you let the vet do everything, it might help you process your grief in a way that makes sense to you. It might be too difficult for you to handle the body yourself and that is okay, so you should respect that in yourself.

Also, this might be the better choice if your cat died from an accident because seeing their body may be too painful for you to experience. It may trigger your grief to a point of not being healthy, and your memories of your cat would, therefore, be unpleasant and not something that you would like to remember.

Option One Cons

Once your veterinarian has the body, you do not know how the body of your cat is going to be handled. Many people don't want their cats in a plastic bag, carried off to a back room, and then disposed of.

This is not to say that your veterinarian would be insensitive, but if you choose to let the veterinarian be the caretaker, ask them to describe their protocol for handling their patients' bodies. You want to be sure this aligns with your beliefs. Total trust in your veterinarian is paramount.

Another con is that if your cat died at home in their sleep, for instance, it might be awkward for you to take their body to the veterinarian's office. It might be less stressful or traumatic if you keep their body at home for a possible backyard burial or you could call a crematorium of choice to make arrangements. (Both of these options we'll be discussing in detail in chapter 8.)

The biggest disadvantage with leaving your cat's body with the vet is that you don't have control and you don't know if your cat is being treated with respect.

Option Two: *You can take your cat home to be buried or to a crematorium.*

Option Two Pros

If you are able to make the choice of being able to take charge of your cat's body and not have your veterinarian do it, I would highly suggest this option.

I recommend this option for the reason that you get to fully control how your cat's body is handled, which can give you a sense of healthy closure, just as it did for Patsy whose story I'm about to share to demonstrate this pro.

Case Study — Patsy and Popcorn

Popcorn was Patsy's buddy for 16 years. The last year of Popcorn's life was very challenging for Patsy because there were so many changes in his health. When it came time to euthanize Popcorn, Patsy was a little confused by her veterinarian's insistence on taking care of Popcorn's body.

Luckily Patsy had just started working with me, and she knew that she wanted to be in charge of caring and being responsible for Popcorn's body. She convinced her veterinarian that she had a plan.

Patsy could not bear to have anyone else handle Popcorn's body. It was very important to her that his body was handled properly, so she and her husband created a cozy spot in the backseat of their car and drove Popcorn to a crematorium.

The crematorium had a special service where they made a paw print in plaster before they cremated Popcorn's body. Patsy keeps the plastered paw print in her kitchen on top of the refrigerator—where Popcorn liked to hang out.

* * *

Here is what happens when you pursue the second option— you get to deal with your loss on another level, one that allows you to actively participate, possibly even have friends help you, all so you can expand your relationship with your loyal cat in an entirely different way. With such active participation, a new form of love fills your heart that directly connects to your cat and your healing.

It also allows you additional time for closure. For example, another client of mine, Amy, decided that she was going to take Patches to the crematorium herself. On her way there, she stopped at her favorite pet supply store and bought Patches his favorite catnip toy. She then gave that toy to him when she surrendered his body to the folks at the crematorium, so the catnip would be processed along with Patches' body.

Plus, it was Amy's final way of saying good-bye to Patches. This helped Amy heal as the months progressed because she had the memory of doing something very sweet for Patches. It is another way of respecting and honoring the relationship that she had with her cat.

This is not to say that you won't experience grief, but what it will give you is memories and a sense that you did everything you could for your cat.

Option Two Cons

Sometimes when you choose to deal with your cat's body yourself, it can be an overwhelming experience to drive your cat home to be buried or to the crematorium.

If you have children at home (something we'll explore in chapter 9 and that I'm addressing exclusively in my next book,) unsupportive family members, it could make the experience of handling your cat's body yourself difficult or unpleasant for you.

The other thing to think about is that if you want to bury your cat in your backyard, the season will factor into the decision. If the ground is frozen, it is difficult to do a backyard burial. If this is the case, you'll want to have a plan on how you are going to preserve the body.

For example, my clients Theresa and her family wanted a backyard burial but it was winter when their beloved cat, River, died, so they brought River home, put her in the freezer, and waited until spring. This may sound gruesome to some, but to Theresa and her family, it was what they wanted to do for River. Doing so helped them manage their grief in a more peaceful and reassuring manner.

Here are some other potential difficulties to consider too:

- You may not have a pet crematorium or cemetery in your area, and it would be difficult for you to transport your cat's body to one in another part of the state or even to a whole different state.

- If you live in an apartment building, you may not have land for a backyard burial.

- The cost of either cremation or burial in a pet cemetery could be prohibitive, so other possibilities would need to be considered.

No matter what your choice is for the handling of your cat's body, keep in mind that it is your choice and you make your decision based on your beliefs, needs, and desires.

Chapter Wrap-Up

In this chapter, I supplied you with information and considerations to help with the decision on how you would like to handle your cat's body. There are many ways to look at this personal choice. The key is to understand what you can handle, what you want to deal with, and what is going to help you feel better.

With the chapter's *Contemplation Questions*, you will explore your own personal beliefs and feelings in order to arrive at the most appropriate decision for you and your cat.

In chapter 8, we are going to talk about the particular variables at play in regard to deciding between a backyard burial, a cremation, or a pet cemetery burial for your beloved cat companion. You will learn about the details of each option and explore which is the best for you.

Chapter 7 Contemplation Questions

1. Do you want your vet to take care of everything? If so, why is that right for you, and how are you going to say good-bye? List the pros and cons that are unique to this choice for you.

2. Do you want to take care of your cat's body yourself? List the pros and cons about this decision for you.

3. Just as Amy stopped at her favorite store to buy a catnip toy as she drove Patches' body to the crematorium, consider a final symbolic gesture that you could do to demonstrate love and respect for your furry pal. Make sure the gesture complements the decision you've made to either ask your vet to handle your cat's body or to handle it yourself.

8. Planning for Burial, Cremation, or Pet Cemetery

For those of you who made the decision not to leave your cat's body with the veterinarian, in this chapter we are going to explore options for handling your cat's remains either through cremation or burial.

The Cremation Option

Many of my clients choose cremation over burial. Everyone has their own unique reasons, but the two most prevalent reasons for cremation are (1) city ordinances in urban communities and (2) they want the ashes of their cat, so they can keep them or sprinkle them in a favorite place as a formal way of saying good-bye.

Case Study — Victoria and Zen-ne

My client Victoria was a cat fancier who showed her cats in pageants around the country. She was a well-respected breeder and has had many cats throughout her life. However, she told me it was Zen-ne that filled her soul. Not only did he win best-in-show three times, but also Zen-ne was the cat that kept her focused on what mattered most in her personal life.

Victoria knew that when Zen-ne died, she would be doing something very special with his ashes. Since they both traveled to shows all over the country, she wanted a little bit of Zen-ne's soul sprinkled at their special places around the country.

One of her favorite places was in Seattle, WA. It was here that Victoria first met Zen-ne and where she liked to go when she needed a break from her busy life. She decided that she was going to visit Seattle with Zen-ne's ashes and leave a little bit at each place she visited that calmed her soul.

When she arrived in Seattle with Zen-ne's ashes, Victoria picked a favorite place each day there and said a little prayer while sprinkling Zen-ne's ashes to say good-bye.

After her return home, Victoria shared with me, "I am very pleased I went to Seattle with Zen-ne's ashes. I felt his spirit and his heart in mine as I said my prayers. Healing my grief this way gave my heart what it needed. I still miss him, but I know his love is strong."

The cremation option is becoming more and more popular with animal-lovers. Since cremation has become more popular, more options are available for you to choose from.

I recommend that you ask your veterinarian which crematorium they use and then make sure to do your own research. You want to be sure you choose a place that has strict ethics and spotless business practices.

How Cremation Works

In pet cremation, your pet is placed in a chamber that is heated between 1400 and 1800 degrees. The heat reduces your pet's remains to basic calcium compounds. In other words, to ashes.

After these ashes cool, they are removed from the chamber and placed in an urn or a container of your choice. You are then able to take them home and keep them with you.

Types of Cremation

Please keep in mind there are different types of cremations for cats.

The first is a *private cremation*. This is one in which your cat's body is the sole body in the cremation chamber, and you will receive the ashes of your cat. This option is the most expensive, and exact fees depend on your geographical area.

The second option is a *viewing cremation*, which is not always available. It is the same as a private cremation but also allows family to be present during the process in a separate viewing room. This option, if available, is less expensive than the private cremation but can have a considerable cost associated with it.

The third option is a *semi-private* or *partitioned cremation*, which allows for multiple pets in the same chamber. Your cat would have their own partition; however, the ashes that you receive would be from all the pets in that chamber, not just from your cat. This alternative is not as expensive as a private cremation but is more costly than the final option.

Please note that the third option can also be considered a *private cremation* at some facilities. I always remind clients to clarify the particularities with the facility they use—and you should do the same. You don't want to risk your cat's ashes mixing with others if that is not what you want or expect.

The final option is a *communal cremation*, which is also known as a *mass* or *batch cremation*. This form of service places multiple animals in the same chamber with no form of separation. No ashes are returned to you. This is the least expensive type of cremation.

Keep in mind that various facilities will have different ways of explaining their services. Again—please ask questions and get clarification if there is something you do not understand.

Personally, I visited two pet crematoriums in my area and asked to see the facilities as well as descriptions of their services. The folks that ran both facilities were very compassionate people and offered other services as well, such as a paw print in plaster, a lock of fur, beautiful urn choices, and an honoring of the request to have a favorite toy or blanket in the chamber with your animal.

When I work with my clients on deciding about cremation, there are some common questions that come up that I would like to share with you. It is understandable you would have questions and concerns surrounding your pet's aftercare.

I stress to my clients that no matter whom you choose to perform this service, be sure to ask the following questions. Also, be a hundred percent satisfied with the answers before you move forward.

Essential Questions to Ask Crematorium Facilities

1. *Who exactly will perform the cremation?*

You want to make sure the person handling your cat's body and handling the cremation furnace is a person of integrity who is experienced at the work—not someone who is unskilled, untrained, overworked, or hates their job. Basically, the pet crematorium industry is not highly regulated at this time, so be prepared to ask them lots of questions about their practices.

2. *How long will I have to wait for the cremation to take place?*

This varies from facility to facility. Some cremations take several weeks; some take several days. The reason for this is that they may be busy with other cremations or only schedule pet cremation on certain days. Make sure you ask them or get an answer from your veterinarian if you leave your cat's body with them.

In my experience, if it takes several days or weeks, you can leave the body at the crematorium. They are equipped for this, and if the facility has high standards, it will take very good care of your cat's body. Again, find out how the body will be cared for in the event you have to wait.

I personally try to choose a crematorium where I can wait and receive my pet's ashes the same day. This way I feel more secure, safe, and at peace.

Knowing how long it will take will help you to manage your stress and, therefore, be less likely to trigger your grief.

3. *How do I know that the ashes I am receiving are my cat's?*

Whether you allow your veterinarian full control or you take your cat's body to the crematorium, ask them how they keep track of the animal remains at their facility. If you don't like the answer, move on. If you do like the response and you trust the individual or organization's answer, this can provide you with peace of mind.

Home Burial

If cremation is not your choice, there is also the option of a home burial. This allows you to bury your cat at home. If you live in an urban area, this might not be allowed, so check that out first. However, if you live in the country, you may opt for a home burial so that you can bury your beloved companion in a favorite spot.

Keep in mind though there are some practical and some difficult things you will encounter and must consider when burying your cat.

It is important to choose your gravesite carefully. Some of my clients pick areas that they loved or that their cats loved—in the garden, under a beautiful tree, or near a rock in the meadow where their cat hunted.

Like Chris and Pudding

Chris buried her cat, Pudding, in Pudding's favorite hunting spot in the backyard. This was a special place because Pudding would ask Chris on a daily basis to come hunting with him, and he always led Chris to his hunting grounds. It made perfect sense after her sweet Pudding died to place him in an area that meant something special.

You will want to choose a place that will not be disturbed in the future. Don't put your cat's gravesite in a wet area, near cables or underground pipes, or even near water sources, such as wells, ponds, and streams. You want an undisturbed, dry area that will be a permanent place for you to visit.

Also consider the size of the gravesite. You will need to dig at least four to five feet down into the ground. This will ensure that other animals will not disturb the burial area or rain will not wash the topsoil away and expose the grave, which could be a very traumatic experience for you.

I also encourage my clients to bury their cats in something that is biodegradable rather than plastic—towels, wood, and cloth are great choices. Try to stay away from plastic caskets or burying them with their favorite bed if it was stuffed with synthetic material.

My clients who choose this option place a stone or a marker at the site, which is a great way to memorialize your cat (we will talk about this more in chapter 12). It also lends to the sacredness of the site.

Pet Cemetery

One of the reasons why you may like to choose a pet cemetery is that if you do a home burial, you may not live at your current home for your entire life. This would mean that if you move, you would not be able to take the body of your pet with you and you may not be welcomed to return to the property to visit the grave.

For this reason, a pet cemetery would provide you with a sacred site to visit and remember your companion.

When choosing a pet cemetery, there are many things to consider. First, be sure that the cemetery is a current member of the International Association of Pet Cemeteries and Crematoriums (IAOPCC.) When you select a pet funeral home, cemetery, or crematorium that is a member, you, as the client, are guaranteed that the provider follows a code of ethics and is of the highest standards. Also, the best way to check if the facility is a current IAOPCC member is by going to the IAOPCC website because some cemeteries and crematoriums will display the logo—as if they are members—without actually belonging.

Unlike human cemeteries, pet cemeteries are not regulated in all states. So be aware of the standards and laws in your individual state.

Things to ask include the following:

1. Who owns the land where the facility is?

2. Are you running out of land for burials?

3. Are there any deed restrictions?

4. Will this land ever be used for something else?

5. How long have you been established?

6. Who owns the facility?

7. Are you a member of the IAOPCC?

8. Who are the employees, and what is their experience?

9. What are the fees?

The other thing to consider is who is going to take your cat to the cemetery. Many cemeteries offer this service as does your veterinarian's office. Your decision will be based on trusting your choice and whether you are emotionally able to transport your cat yourself.

In my experience, every pet cemetery is different in the way that they provide services for their clients. Price ranges vary according to location.

The best thing to do is find a pet cemetery in your area that is registered with the IAOPCC and ask the questions above that I gave you. Make sure they are a trusted and well-respected business.

Then if you are happy with their answers, you can go a step further and ask them specific questions about costs, etc.

Here are some things to consider when speaking to the staff at the pet cemetery of your choice:

1. What are my choices and prices for the gravesite of my cat?

2. Do you offer transportation of my cat's body from my home or from my veterinarian's office?

3. Do you offer individual plots or are your plots communal?

4. Who takes care of the general maintenance of my cat's gravesite? Are there extra fees?

5. Am I allowed to come visit the gravesite whenever I want?

6. Do you offer funeral services?

7. Can I leave toys, flowers, and mementos at my cat's gravesite?

Pet cemeteries can provide you with caskets, headstones, and burial site maintenance. Just be clear and prepared if you go with this option about all the costs involved.

As a pet funeral celebrant, I have been asked to lead various pet funerals and memorial services in some amazing pet cemeteries that were beautifully cared for and maintained. Yet, there have been some that I questioned. Do your research and be sure the pet cemetery of your choice meets your criteria.

Chapter Wrap-Up

In this chapter, you learned of ways that you can respectfully take care of your cat's body. You learned how to research a crematorium and about the cremation process. You also have some questions to ask when considering a crematorium. If cremation is not your choice, you learned of two burial options that may suit your needs instead, as well as important considerations for each of these.

With the *Contemplation Questions* at the end of this chapter, you will get a chance to explore how you feel about cremation or burial to help you become clearer about your choice.

Chapter 9 will be helpful to you if you have children of your own or if there were children in your cat's life that will miss your cat. While death in our society can be a difficult topic, teaching a child about pet loss is important for building honesty and resilience.

Chapter 8 Contemplation Questions

1. Are you trying to decide between cremation and burial? Do some research that will help you decide. Research the crematorium and pet cemetery options in your area. Also, find out about your locality's rules on burying pets at home.

2. How do you feel about cremation? If you choose cremation, what questions would you ask your veterinarian and/or crematorium?

3. Have you considered a home burial? If so, where would that be? How would you mark the gravesite?

9. Supporting Children with Pet Loss

In our society death is a very difficult topic, and for the most part we would all like to avoid it. Yet, death is part of life. When teaching your child about pet loss, it is important to know your feelings and attitudes about death first. If you are unclear about these, your confused or vague explanation of death could, in turn, affect the way your child views loss in the future.

As an adult, you know there is an end to all life. The thing to remember is that even though you understand that all living things die, the death of your cat may be the first time your child, or a child in your cat's life, encounters death. What this means is that your child will likely experience new, and perhaps difficult, feelings.

Since children are naturally curious and want to know how things work, they will experience various stages of grief and loss that could be extremely difficult for them to comprehend. However, this could be the perfect opportunity to teach them about life and death, and help them be more resilient as they age.

Guidelines for Supporting a Child

Your child will look to you to help them through their feelings of grief and mourning, to help them understand that death is normal. There are many ways that you can help your child understand the loss of their pet.

These five tips are the guidelines that I use with my clients when they are looking for additional support with children. In using these five tips, you will create a healthy, positive atmosphere and experience for your child.

Tip 1—*Honesty is critical when talking about death to your child.*

If you are unclear about your feelings about death, it will be difficult to be honest. However, it is important to tell your child the truth. Avoid half-truths, generalizations, or the use of clichés or myths (chapter 3).

Your child will ask questions about where their cat went, whether their cat will come back, and why the death happened. By answering with clear and informative responses, you will help them to develop a healthy attitude.

It is important to tell them that their cat has not gone to sleep, run away, or is living on a farm. Depending on the age of your child, you will be crafting your response according to their level of development.

Be clear, honest, and talk about death in simple and specific terms.

For example, if your child is five years old or younger, you could say, "Gilbert died. His body just stopped working. He has stopped eating, moving, seeing, and hearing. We are all going to miss him."

This was exactly what my client Sahara told her son Zach when Gilbert, their cat, died. They did it this way to lessen Zach's fear. They had to tell Zach this same message about Gilbert's death repeatedly, but it helped Zach grasp the fact that his cat died. It didn't scare him or foster myths or untruths about life and death.

By eight or nine, children are able to grasp the meaning of death, so it will be appropriate to explain it in more adult terms. Knowing how you feel about death and the grieving process will help you craft meaningful explanations for your child.

For example, Joanne and Mike told their son Jason the following when he asked how long Beeker was going to live:

> Beeker's body hurts, and he is very old. Beeker has trouble eating, so he is not getting the nutrients he needs. His illness is making him very sick. So instead of letting him suffer any longer, it is time to let him die. Remember, how I explained that to you? We will take Beeker to the vet, and the vet will give him medication that will help him do this.

Tip 2—*Carefully allow your emotions of grief to show in front of your child.*

As you know, full honesty is important when explaining death to your child. Even still, keep in mind that since the emotions of grief may be new for your child, when they observe your emotions, this experience will affect them.

When your emotions are heightened, it is okay to share them with your child. You loved the family cat, and your emotions are important to express and understand. Depending on the age of your child, the death of their cat is going to bring on feelings that they have not experienced before.

Your feelings of grief, such as crying and being sad, are normal when losing a beloved cat and are important to share. When you show these feelings to your child, it will help them understand that their grief feelings are normal too. Yet, if you become raging with anger or extremely depressed, those emotions may not be healthy for your child to experience at this time. Extreme emotions of grief are better to express without your child observing.

Joanne and Mike oftentimes had to go into their bedroom to express their most challenging grief emotions when Jason was at home from school. They both knew that it was important to only let Jason see healthy grief emotions, so they wouldn't frighten him. However, when they expressed their sorrow in front of Jason, they both felt comfortable with gentle expressions of what they were feeling.

Tip 3—*Help, guide, and support your child through their feelings of grief.*

Once you know and understand what the common feelings of grief are (chapters 1 and 2), share them with your child and allow your child to talk about them with you. Your child will probably have many questions, so be prepared to talk to them and explain to them what happens during the end-of-life period.

Joanne and Mike did this with Jason. She took the list in this book and showed it to Jason. They talked about each item on the list and how it made them feel. She answered Jason's questions and let him know that his feelings were important.

Tip 4—*Grief and mourning are different.*

When you create the time for your child to ask questions and express grief, it will provide a time for you and your family to lovingly create another level of closeness and bonding. Grief is an inward expression of suffering from a loss, and mourning is the outward expression (more in chapter 11). It is so important to allow your child, and really everyone closely connected to your valued cat, to outwardly express their inner grief with a pet funeral or pet memorial that they help design.

When your child can express their ideas, thoughts, and suggestions, they will know that you support them fully. It will help them with their feelings of grief, teach them about losses in life, and help them to develop into adaptable, capable, and functional adults.

In chapter 12, we will talk about how to create life celebrations that will help not only you but also your child to have a healthy and valuable experience participating in this part of life with your cherished cat.

Tip 5—*Be an example for how to move through the grieving process.*

Since the death of your family's cat may be the first experience your child will have surrounding death and grief, understanding your own attitude and reactions is critical.

There are many myths that surround death that we covered in chapter 3. When you explore these myths, they can help you understand and process your feelings. Also, understanding that grief has a life of its own that can surface at unexpected times will help you be prepared for your child's question, fears, and feelings.

Knowing what normal grief is as opposed to abnormal grief will guide you to a clearer perspective so that you can be fully aware and present for your child during this difficult time (chapters 1 and 2).

Since this is may be your child's first exposure to death, know that they probably will not know how to respond or why they have the feelings that they do.

This experience gives you the opportunity to be a confidant, teacher, supporter, and role model who is there for them, listens, and unconditionally loves them, just as your treasured cat did.

For greater guidance in the area of supporting children when a beloved pet dies, you may want to consult my next book entitled *Pets as Compassionate Teachers of Pet Loss: A Comprehensive Guide for Parents of Children Who Are Facing the Loss of Their Pet*. This book is for parents who are looking for a no-nonsense approach to teach their child about life, death, and beyond in an easy and concise manner. At the end of this book, I give an extensive description of the topics my next book addresses.

Chapter Wrap-Up

In this chapter, you learned why pets are so important and how they can be incredible teachers for introducing death to a child. With the five tips provided, you will be able to support your child in their first encounter with death and be the perfect role model for this life experience.

With the chapter's *Contemplation Questions* below, you will begin to organize your plan of action on how to help your child.

In the next chapter, you will explore a very common issue concerning the right time to get another cat. Most of my clients go through varying levels of anguish about inviting another cat into their lives after the deaths of their beloved companions. You will hear the stories of Angela and Azia. Plus, you will receive eight tips to help you with this decision.

Chapter 9 Contemplation Questions

1. What are your feelings about death? Can you make a list? Do you consider each of your feelings about death healthy?

2. How will you tell your child about death when they ask about the death of their cat?

3. Are there any comments that you made that may be half-true, vague, or considered to be myths? If so, can you change them to reflect a clear and honest answer?

10. Loving Another Cat

Determining when to get another cat can be an excruciating decision for you. This decision oftentimes has people going back and forth, never seeming to reach a decision they feel a hundred percent confident about.

Unfortunately, the loss of our cats is inescapable since their lifespans are not as long as ours. Still, it doesn't lessen the pain of loss in any way. Your grief is still going to be felt, and you are going to feel alone if you don't have other critters in your household.

For some of my clients, opening their heart to a new cat to invite into their home right after their companion dies is extremely helpful. Yet, for other clients, it can take a long time before they are ready. For some, they never are able to have another cat because the pain is so intense.

Remember in chapters 1 and 2 when I talked about how grief has a life of its own? How grief is unique to you and everyone is different in how they process their grief? Similarly, making a decision to get another cat is a personal choice for you to make.

My client Angela and her family couldn't imagine a home without a cat, and they remedied it very quickly after their Apricot died. They couldn't stand coming home and not having the cheerful meows of Apricot running towards them, welcoming them home. To Angela, getting a new cat quickly eased her distress and brought happiness. For her, it was the right choice.

Yet my client Azia needed to grieve her loss of Curry much longer before she felt ready to adopt another cat. She felt that she needed the time to grieve so that she could work through her feelings without having a new cat to distract her.

For Azia, this was the sensible thing to do because she wanted to be sure that she didn't "replace" Curry or express grief in front of her new cat. She also didn't want to feel disloyal to Curry by opening her heart to another cat.

While some people are like Angela and want a new cat right away and other people are like Azia and want to wait a while before they are ready, there are others that have no timeframe at all. They make the choice to wait as long as it takes until the right cat comes along.

Most of my clients go through varying levels of anguish about inviting another cat into their lives after the death of their beloved companion. It is a very common feeling, and it is normal. By reading the story of Angela and Azia, I hope you will be able to trust where you are at with your journey of grief to make the best decision for you.

8 Tips to Keep in Mind

1. When welcoming another cat into your family, no matter where you are with your grief, this action can trigger feelings of loss that you thought you had already dealt with. It can challenge you to deal with grief feelings on a deeper level, which can be uncomfortable, surprising, and uninvited.

2. There is no right or wrong time to bring another cat into your life. It's really up to you. There are some things to consider to be sure that you are truly ready, but there are no hard-and-fast rules for making this decision.

3. Try not to make a hasty decision. Give yourself time to grieve and think. Don't let anyone tell you what the right decision is or pressure you into getting a cat.

4. Your new cat should not be considered a "replacement" for your previous cat. Replacement relationships are not healthy, and when you build a new relationship with a new cat, your memories and experiences will be different, unique, and very special to the two of you.

5. It is important to involve all family members in the decision to invite a new cat into the household. In particular, consider the needs and feelings of your children. They can easily feel that having a new pet in the home can be disloyal to the previous cat. Everyone in the family needs to have their chance to properly grieve.

6. Since your new cat begins a new relationship with you, it can be very difficult to heal your grief by naming the new cat the same as your previous cat's name. Try and come up with a new name that reflects the personality of the cat and their special antics, personality, characteristics, etc.

7. Having the expectation that your new cat will learn, do, respond, or have the same character traits as your previous cat is not respectful to your new cat. As an alternative, enjoy your new cat as a unique being with a ton of love, fun, and enjoyment to give you. Be excited by the differences and quirkiness.

8. If you have other pets in the house, consider whether they will enjoy or resent a new cat. Some cats mourn the loss of a companion, so it will be important for their health and well-being to support the grief of the surviving cat.

Similarly, to the case studies in this chapter and the *8 Tips to Keep in Mind*, whether to get a new cat really depends on how comfortable you are with the stage of grief that you are at (chapter 2) and if you feel that your grief no longer affects the way you experience your daily life.

When my clients tell me they were at the humane society and found the perfect cat, yet they still question if the time is right, I remind them to step back, take a breath, and trust what they are feeling in their hearts. If there is confusion or doubt, it may mean they are still not ready, and that is okay. But, if the "heart-melt" overcomes the uncertainty, then it may be the perfect time.

Finally, if you are not convinced that you are ready for a new cat, there is always the option to volunteer at your humane society or local rescue group. You would be able to spend time cuddling, socializing, and maybe even fostering a cat in need. You will be able to share the love in your heart and receive comfort in knowing that you are doing something good. This is an excellent way to discover a new furry companion when you least expect it!

Chapter Wrap-Up

In this chapter, you learned how to explore and feel confident about when you are ready to bring another cat into your home. You understand the importance of knowing where you are in your stages of grief and how this can affect your decision. Plus, you received *8 Tips to Keep in Mind* when contemplating your decision.

You heard the stories of Angela and Azia, and how they carefully tuned in to their nuances of grief to determine the right time to get another cat.

With the three *Contemplation Questions*, you will be able to begin the process of knowing when you are ready to bring another cat into your life and how you will go about finding the cat that melts your heart!

In the next chapter, you are going to begin exploring the topic of ways to celebrate the life you had with your cat. We will begin chapter 11 by exploring the difference between "grief" and "mourning."

Chapter 10 Contemplation Questions

1. Are you ready to get another cat now? If so, list the reasons why. After making your list, do you still feel like you are ready?

2. If you are not ready to welcome another cat into your life now, can you list the reasons why? Can you change those reasons into positive statements that help you process your feelings of grief?

3. How do you see your process of inviting another cat into your home unfolding? What does that look like? Will you rescue, foster, volunteer, or something else?

CELEBRATIONS OF LIFE FOR HEALING: SECTION THREE

All the art of living lies in a fine mingling of letting go and holding on.

—Havelock Ellis

11. Deciding on Mourning

For many of us, the words "grief" and "mourning" have been used interchangeably to mean the same thing. However, they are quite different. Knowing that difference will help you with your own journey of healing your grief over losing your furry companion.

As you learned in chapters 1 and 2, grief is your emotional reaction or physical response to your unique loss. Grief can be experienced as shock, confusion, anger, depression, sadness, anxiety, and more.

If you allow your grief to be felt and you accept that grief is normal, your journey to peace gradually changes. Your grief is your body's way of dealing with an event that you may not be able to fully process in that moment. It takes time for your soul to process grief, so please be patient with yourself.

If the death of your cat was sudden or totally unexpected, your struggle may take some time to completely understand. Conversely, if your cat was ill and suffering for a while, the time that you need to process your grief may unfold quite differently.

The important thing to remember is that the loss of your cat is not entirely about losing your companion that you love dearly. It takes into consideration your dreams of what you hold precious and endearing in everyday life. For this reason, it is crucial that you give yourself "permission" to feel your loss and give yourself the space to heal your heart.

Case Study — Lucy and Shadow

Lucy found that with the loss of her cat Shadow it was much easier to endure her grief by not wishing that her pain would go away. Lucy told me, "I was burying my emotions by wishing they would go away because I thought the way to peace was to wish for difficult feelings to stop bothering me. I fooled myself thinking they went away, but then they would show up at unexpected times and remind me of the agony I felt. When I understood this and felt comfortable admitting and then expressing my grief, it finally started to feel like my feelings had a voice to express."

For Lucy, she talked about the pain of Shadow's death to a supportive pet loss grief group and also during our weekly calls. She discovered how important it was to keep talking and feeling. She sought out people in her daily life that would allow her to express her grief feelings, like guilt and anger. She fully participated in her mourning period by sharing her feelings with those that did not judge her.

* * *

Keep in mind that your grief could get derailed if someone gives you a timeline of expectations. "You should be better by now. It has been six months" or "Why are you still feeling so guilty?" If you listen to these statements, as well as the other myths from chapter 3, you may not have the necessary time to mourn and you may get distracted from your journey. Lucy, in her "quest" for supportive people, quickly learned how to include select people in her grief journey (and exclude others!).

Your journey will vary and be different from anyone else's. The pressure to "get better quickly" is one to stay away from. It will ultimately guide you away from the peace that you may be seeking. Feelings do take a while to process.

You will probably never completely lose your feeling of sadness about the loss of your cat, but with time, the frequency and intensity will change. In fact, by allowing your grief to speak and express itself as a remedy for your pain, your healing will come about in time.

On Mourning

The mourning of your cat is the next step. You may not feel like it makes any sense right now, or you may feel that it is impossible to go to this next step; however, mourning is a very beautiful and sacred time for you.

You learned that grief is the internal expression of losing your cat. Mourning is the opposite. It is the outward expression of your grief. We can go deeper and say that mourning is the outside process that you choose to undergo in order to cope with the intense void that you are experiencing on the inside.

When you are ready to mourn, the reflection and introspection of the life you shared with your cherished cat can be very strong and profound. It is the time to love even more deeply and remember that sweet and endearing connection that you shared with your cat that you deeply miss.

This experience will help you as you begin to create a celebration of your cat's life (chapter 12) and while you start to anticipate the changes in your own life (chapter 14).

Remembering, expressing and being open to developing a new clarity will allow you to gain insight into and empathy for your new life. Although this time can be extremely painful and difficult, your grief and mourning process can reveal some amazing gifts that aid you in understanding who you are. Your cat was a teacher. This is the time period to fully reflect on those lessons.

Like grieving, mourning can be a difficult time. Yet, both are necessary for healing pet loss. By walking the journey of pet loss grief and creating a special ceremony that honors the life you had with your pet, you can learn so much and gain a tremendous gift from the experience.

Your animal devoted themselves to you and you to them. The physical loss of that deserves to be mourned. Managing your grief through this period can give you some amazing insight in relation to what your bond truly meant.

Chapter Wrap-Up

In this chapter, you learned that both grief and mourning have different roles in your journey of healing the loss of your beloved feline companion. Even though they can overlap and have no timeframe, your outward expression of your grief (i.e., mourning) will be an invaluable learning tool and a beautiful, sacred time.

With the chapter's *Contemplation Questions*, you will reflect on your own mourning experience and discover how mourning is actually the remedy to heal your pain.

In chapter 12, you will learn of actual ways to express your grief through some mourning rituals. When you are ready to approach healing your pet loss with a pet funeral, pet memorial, pet remembrance, and/or an end-of-life celebration, chapter 12 will guide you.

Chapter 11 Contemplation Questions

1. Both grief and mourning are important and valuable for healing the pain of losing your cat. With guidance from previous chapters, what are you experiencing in your grief journey? Are you now ready to mourn? If so, how? If not, what is holding you back?

2. How can mourning heal your body, mind, and spirit?

3. Can you list ways that you will be compassionate and patient with yourself during your mourning?

12. Appreciating Your Cat's Life

Grief is different from mourning, and you can easily get caught up with your grief and forget to outwardly express your feelings, which is what it means to mourn. Learning how to express your grief and mourn the loss of your cat is an important step when healing your pet loss. Mourning is a way of saying good-bye in a very healthy way.

In this chapter, you are going to explore the different ways in which you can both mourn and celebrate your cat's life—through a pet funeral or other type of end-of-life celebration. If you are ready for something different yet extremely beneficial for your heart and soul, the celebrations that I am going to share with you in this chapter provide new ways of respecting and honoring your cat.

Since you are a very special person that wants to honor your highly valued cat, please remember that if someone tells you that you are strange for holding an end-of-life ceremony for your cat—PLEASE DON'T LISTEN! If you listen, you will be holding back a very important step for healing your grief.

By going through the necessary process of mourning (chapter 11) and exploring the options in this chapter, you will have the chance to respectfully celebrate the life of your cat and thank them for everything they did for you. In celebrating your cat, you honor that special relationship you both had, thus providing a positive and healthy outlet for your grief.

Also, by spending time creating the end-of-life ceremony yourself or by having a pet funeral celebrant help you create a personalized celebration, you will get the chance to have some closure and say good-bye. I have been conducting pet funerals and pet memorials for many years, and I have found that the value of holding a commemorative event is an invaluable aid in the healing process. Expressing your feelings and showing tribute to your cat is healthy, normal, and essential.

Case Study — Carol, Hans & Tigger

My clients Carol and Hans hired me to design and conduct a backyard celebration when their cat Tigger died. I worked with them to compose a beautiful eulogy that paid tribute to all the things that they shared with Tigger.

It was a small and beautiful celebration that honored Tigger with great respect and compassion.

It was a special day for Carol and Hans—the weather was perfect. Hans even said before I read the eulogy that it was the type of weather that Tigger loved. When I read the eulogy, there were tears and smiles demonstrating the love and support for the relationship that Carol and Hans had with Tigger. It was beautiful to witness the compassion and support their family showed too.

Let me share with you Tigger's eulogy.

Eulogy for Tigger

Hello, everyone. As some as you know, Tigger was a beautiful soul that offered Carol and Hans many years of joy when they adopted him from a shelter. Carol and Hans have asked me to share with you a few stories as we remember what a character Tigger was to his family.

When Tigger first came home with Carol and Hans, he was not in great shape. He was hungry, had fleas, and was clearly neglected. Yet, there was a spark in his eyes that warmed Carol and Hans' heart, and they were going to do everything they could to provide for Tigger. What they didn't expect as Tigger got well was that he had an extreme passion to sit on Carol or Hans' shoulder and purr happily in their ear. One could say he was quite pleased with himself in this position and would perch on Carol or Hans' shoulder as they moved about their day.

After a few years Tigger started to seek out shoulders of friends that came to visit. In fact, if there was a vacant shoulder to perch on, he would be sure to oblige and hop on for the ride, purring all the way . . . Tigger would jump off whatever comfortable spot he was on, claim his next perch, and then proceed to purr softly into the chosen ear!

Even as Tigger got older, Carol and Hans made sure Tigger's favorite shoulders came to visit. He would wait for them to settle down on the couch or the kitchen chair, and he would place himself high on his perch, muzzle to ear, and purr content thoughts.

Anyone who had the opportunity to be the chosen shoulder knew that Tigger had a special message for them. Carol and Hans knew it was the unconditional love that a cat has for its family and friends.

Thank you, Tigger, for being there for Carol and Hans, and for being their trusted companion. Thank you for comforting their friends. You were an angel disguised as a black cat with white patches!

After the ceremony, Hans shared with me, "Wendy, this was so lovely. I am so glad we had a funeral for Tigger. I could feel him sitting on my shoulder while you read the eulogy. I feel like a deep hole in my heart has been softened. I know it will still be painful at times, but I also have this beautiful memory that I celebrated the life we shared with him."

Types of Celebrations

Here are possibilities for the types of end-of-life celebrations that you can consider when you are ready for this step in healing your pet loss. I list them here and will talk more about them later in this chapter.

Pet Funeral—This is a celebration/service in which the body or cremains of your cat are present. This event takes place relatively soon after your cat reaches the end of their life.

Pet Memorial—This is the celebration/service in which the body or cremains of your cat are not present. This event can take place whenever you so choose. There is no time limit as to when a pet memorial takes place.

Pet Remembrances—These are the anniversaries, holidays, and/or special occasions that you shared with your cat during which you celebrate the memory of them.

The Resulting Rewards

The thing that I absolutely love about planning and officiating a pet funeral or memorial service is that I get to witness the unwavering amount of love and healing that takes place.

Even though there is much sadness, there are moments of incredibly rich emotional sharing in the celebration of a cat's life. I witness life-changing events that people undergo by sharing aloud about their life with their cherished cat. I feel honored to be part of those tender moments shared by those who miss their cat and are mourning the loss of their treasured family member.

These are some of those life-changing moments that a pet funeral or memorial service can provide to support the griever in their journey of healing pet loss grief. A pet funeral, pet memorial, or pet remembrance can provide:

- a sense of reality that your pet has reached the end of their life;

- the opportunity for friends and family members to share their thoughts, experiences, and feelings;

- the space for you and others to acknowledge, reflect, and honor the incredible role that the animal played in your lives; and/or

- a healthy way to say a formal good-bye.

A *pet funeral* is generally held within a few days of your cat's death and may consist of a viewing, a formal service, and a brief rite at the gravesite. The atmosphere is usually somber and sad, and the emphasis is on death, mourning, and loss.

The funeral can be held at a pet cemetery or in your backyard if your local ordinances allow this. You may invite family, friends, and anyone else that supports your journey and respects your cat and the special relationship you had with your cat. The ceremony you create can include music, a celebration after the service, and time for others to share their feelings about your dear cat.

A *memorial service*, on the other hand, may be held at any time after your cat's death. Its function is to remember and celebrate your cat's life. Oftentimes, the mood is more positive and uplifting. The service can be as small and private, or as open and elaborate, as you wish, and it can be delayed as long as its planning requires. Keep in mind, however, that having the service closer to the time when your loss is most deeply felt is when it is most likely to help you and your family express and work through grief.

Many of my clients who choose cremation also choose a memorial service that includes spreading the ashes at a favorite locale that their cat loved. Many times a eulogy is also included, as well as a celebration with food afterwards.

Just like a funeral, your memorial service will reflect your unique relationship with your cat and will include those elements that are meaningful to you.

Pet remembrances are lifelong celebrations. Every year, you can celebrate your cat's birthday by lighting a candle and having a small ceremony. You can also go to your cat's gravesite and leave a favorite toy. You may even want to go to a special place that you and your cat loved and spend a few moments of silence to remember their presence.

Every year I encourage my clients to go to a special place that they shared with their cat and read to them a love letter (chapter 13) that expresses their love for their cat who has died.

Important Points for Planning

Here are some points you may wish to consider as you plan your own unique ceremony of remembrance for your cat:

- Take some time to plan what you'd like to do. Involve all family members (including children) and others who support you and who are willing to help.

- Consider whether you want to hold a funeral, a memorial service, or both.

- Given your religious beliefs, traditions, and rituals, determine whether you want to include any religious aspects or whether you consider their inclusion inappropriate.

- Think of ways the service can be personalized. Ask family members and friends who knew your pet to reminisce with you and recall what was special about your pet.

- Decide who will hold the service, where, when it will be held, who will speak, and who will be invited to attend.

- If you're working with a representative of a pet cemetery or crematory, ask if you can view your pet beforehand and hold the service then.

- Find out what other grieving pet owners have done to honor their pets' memories. Think of ways you can adapt their ideas to make them your own.

- Know that it is both normal and healthy to use a funeral or memorial service to express your sorrow, proclaim your love, and bid a final farewell to your cherished friend.

Chapter Wrap-Up

In this chapter, we explored why it is important to celebrate your cat's life with a pet funeral, memorial, and/or remembrance. You learned the difference between the three and heard the story of Carol and Hans and how much having a pet funeral for Tigger helped them on their grief journey. Plus, I supplied you with some important points for planning end-of-life ceremonies.

With the chapter's *Contemplation Questions*, you will be able to begin to create your own pet funeral, memorial, and/or remembrance that is special to you and reflects the life that you shared with your cat.

In the next chapter, you are going to learn of a beautiful and extremely healing exercise—writing a love letter to your cat—that can help you keep your cat in your heart and soul.

Chapter 12 Contemplation Questions

1. How would you like to celebrate your cat's life—a funeral, memorial, and/or remembrance?

2. Would you include other people? If so, make a list of whom you would invite. Consider if you will ask anyone to speak.

3. Are you going to write the eulogy yourself? If so, what will you include?

13. Writing a Love Letter

One of the most important exercises that I share with my clients who are experiencing deep pain and heartache after their cat has died is writing a love letter to their cat to express how much they love them.

A love letter provides a very special way of healing your grief. It is a different way to tell your cat how much you love them. It is a way to express your memories, experiences, and gratitude for the things that you shared with your beloved feline.

Your mind clutter may be a little chaotic with all your thoughts and feelings at this point. Remember—that is okay. It doesn't matter where you are in your grief journey because writing a love letter to your cat at any time is a wonderful way to heal pet grief.

No matter where you are with your unique feelings of pet grief, having one place where you can collect and express the love that you have for your cat is extremely helpful. When you can bring together and express your special love bond that you had with your cat in a love letter, it is extremely therapeutic. In writing this letter, you can deepen the connection you had with your furry companion and make a statement of your incredible bond.

Are you not sure where to begin? Are you not really clear how to go about this love letter? That is okay because I am going to help you. I encourage you to spend some time every day jotting down special memories or things that you want to tell your cat—even if it is only five to ten minutes a day that you spend writing. Doing so will lead to your writing a personal love letter to your cat.

This letter will be an accumulation of love and thanks from you to your beloved companion. It is your proclamation of appreciation, healing, apology (if needed), and inclusion of anything else that you may want to express to your dearly loved cat now that they are no longer physically in your life. It is your way to say good-bye in a meaningful way.

My clients who work with me in my Rescue Joy from Pet Loss Grief program have found healing and solace when they write love letters. In the course, my clients write a series of letters that help them cope with pet loss with grace, respect, and compassion for themselves.

You may be asking, "Why write things down? Why write a love letter? How is that going to help me?" These are common questions, and oftentimes writing is not one of the favorite activities for my clients—until they write the first letter and discover how healing it can be.

Case Study — Melanie and Mister

Melanie discovered the positive, restorative rewards when she wrote a love letter to her soul kitty cat Mister. Melanie discovered that this exercise provided very healing means to express her grief and tell Mister how much he meant to her. By writing down her thoughts and expressing herself,

Melanie found great solace to mourn the deep pain that she felt.

Melanie wrote many letters to Mister, and by writing, she recalled and recaptured the amazing life she'd had with him. She learned many important things about herself and came to clearly recognize the loving gifts that Mister gave her.

Melanie's Love Letter to Mister

Dear Mister,

Things that make my soul soar: You made me happy every time I laid eyes on you, every time I knew I was coming home to you. I miss your little/big soul very much. More than I can possibly express.

I have the utmost respect, love, appreciation, gratefulness, and passion for you. I will cherish each memory with heartfelt joy and truth forever.

I pray that our souls meet again very soon. I wasn't done giving you all the love I had/have for you. There is so much more to give to you still.

These are the things I loved/love about you Mister (Magic.) The way you feel, look, smell, cry to go out into the hallway to play, eat, poop and pee, hit me, look at me, walk, run, roll over, sit, sleep, wink, brush your own face with your favorite brushes, rub up against the neighbors' doors, watch the mail go down the shoot, the sound of you crunching on your food, blink your eyes with me, change the size of your pupils, fall back from the sitting position, your furry mops on your hands and feet, lie in the shoebox in the closet, curl up into a baby ball of grey fur with your head tucked under and upside down, sound when you are walking, take a deep breath when you jump up on my bed, lift your front paws in the air before you pounce on your toys, watch me with your eyes only as I walk back and forth, and how much love you gave me.

Mister, saving you was my greatest accomplishment. We nursed each other back to health. We were each other's lifelines, and I am forever grateful. You gave me a reason to live. Thank you, Mister.

Love always, Mom

As her words demonstrate, Melanie experienced this exercise as a powerful and healing declaration of her growth and a processing of her grief in a healthy way. Writing a love letter and then reading it out loud helped her with any lingering feelings of pet grief, such as guilt, denial, and anxiety. Plus, it gave her an overwhelming feeling that she was demonstrating a deep and profound respect for Mister.

Questions to Help Frame Your Love Letter

Each week, I give my clients ten to twelve questions that encourage and support them in choosing a unique way to celebrate the life of their cat. These questions will support you by helping you to determine the feelings of compassion and love that you have for your cat.

Before you answer these questions, have a designated place where you will write your answers. It may be a special journal, your computer, or just a piece of paper. Whatever you choose, be sure to keep all of your answers in one place so that when you are ready to write your love letter, you have everything in front of you.

1. Describe your experience when you first brought your cat home. What happened? How did you feel?

2. Make a list of everything that you and your cat did together. What was the weather like? Where were you? How old were you and your cat? What exactly were you doing? Are there some things that you forgot and remembered again?

3. What was the biggest gift that your cat gave you?

4. Do you have any feelings of guilt or sorrow for something you did or didn't do for your cat? How would you apologize to them beyond just saying, "I am sorry"?

There is no need to answer these questions all at once unless you are really motivated to do so. In fact, each one of these questions can be dedicated to a single love letter.

When you answer these questions, keep in mind that no one else is going to read what you write. Write whatever comes to your mind without judgment and editing. The vital part of this exercise is to get your feelings out on paper so that you are ready to write your love letter with ease.

After you answer all the questions above and maybe some of your own, let your journal sit for a couple of days. You may find you forgot something and want to add it. A memory of you and your cat cuddled up on the couch, strolling through the garden, or sleeping all cuddled up in bed might come back to you.

Keep in mind that this letter doesn't have to be perfect. You can write as many letters as you want. Your cat doesn't mind that you spelled something wrong or that your sentence isn't complete.

The more that you can give back to them, the better you are going to feel. Keep in mind this mourning exercise is not time sensitive. If you just lost your cat or it has been months or even years, writing a love letter to them at any time is extremely helpful with processing your grief. Many of my clients still write letters to all of their cats, and with each one, they learn something new about the relationship and themselves.

Time to Write

After you think you have everything down that you want to tell your cat, it is now time to take out a fresh piece of paper or open a new word document and write your love letter.

The first thing to do is put the date on the top of your letter. The reason for this is that sometime in the future, whether it is months or years from now, you will probably come across the letter. The date will help you put in perspective where you were, and where you now are, in coping with your pet loss grief.

Then start your letter with "Dear [Name of your cat]." I recommend beginning the letter with your cat's given name rather than a nickname because using their given name allows you to have a conversation that is equal and respectful. Also, you can always include any nicknames in the body of the letter.

Next, you start telling your cat all those things that you brainstormed and recorded in response to the questions. If you find that it is difficult to write just one letter, do as many as you want.

The time that you spend on your letter is up to you. Some of my clients spend a little time writing each day for a few days, and some will write their entire letters in one sitting. No matter how you go about it, get the letter done. You will be so happy that you did.

After your letter is written, go to a special place where you are comfortable. It might be a special place that you and your furry feline friend shared together in nature. It might be at the pet cemetery where your cat is buried (chapter 8), or it may be lying in bed with your cat's favorite toy beside you.

I suggest you do this alone so that you can give your grief and your letter full attention without worrying what someone else thinks of you, your letter, or the fact that you are reading it aloud.

It doesn't matter what others think of your pet grief journey. If you cry, just remember, you are experiencing some tough grief here. This entire book is dedicated to supporting you so that you don't feel weird, crazy, or isolated because you are grieving the loss of your cat.

Chapter Wrap-Up

In this chapter, we talked about how your relationship with your cat was unique. Your cat loved you, and you loved your cat. Cherish that, write them a love letter, go to a special spot when you read it aloud, and feel good about how you are walking this journey of pet loss grief.

The *Contemplation Questions* will continue to guide you through the process of writing and reading your love letter to your cat.

In chapter 14, I am going to continue to support you with your pet grief by including information on what you can expect in your life after your cat has died. We will explore how you can plan for ways in which your life will be different and how you can cope with this.

Chapter 13 Contemplation Questions

1. In what ways do you think that writing a letter to your cat will help you heal your grief?

2. How do you feel happy and joyful when you write down the memories that you shared with your companion?

3. Now that you have written and read your letter to your cat, have any of your feelings of grief lessened or changed? Write that down, so you can reflect on those changes and feel good about them.

14. Accepting Your New Normal

In this chapter, I am going to continue to support you during another perplexing and possibly challenging time of adjustment for you—your "new normal."

What is your "new normal?" It basically means who you are without your cat—your thoughts, decisions, and changes in outlook in regard to your life.

We will explore what you can expect after your cat has reached the end of their life and they are no longer physically with you. I will share some examples of how your life will change after your cat dies and how you can cope with these changes.

My goal is to continue to help you through this difficult time. I want to give you as many tools as I can so that you feel supported throughout your journey and know what to expect.

Let's begin with a case study in which we learn about Tracey's transition to her "new normal" after her loss of Luis.

Case Study — Tracey and Luis

Tracey had a very difficult time with the death of Luis. He was her life and came into her life when Tracey had just divorced her husband. Her heart was empty, and she knew that bringing Luis into her life would be a healing experience.

Every day Tracey and Luis had a routine that they both enjoyed, beginning with Tracey's yoga practice. Luis liked to sit next to Tracey as she went through her yoga sequence— purring and flicking his tail.

Tracey shared with me, "Without Luis there with me during yoga practice, I'm finding it hard to continue the practice. If I do, I feel like it disrespects the bond I shared with him. I am getting tired of people around me telling me that I have been sad long enough and I need to get back to my yoga practice and my life."

Here is the thing about what Tracey was experiencing— everything that she said is considered normal grief. She experienced a very huge loss in her life. Through the act of articulating what she felt was challenging and important in her life without Luis, Tracey was beginning to discover her "new normal."

When Tracey was ready, I shared with her the following five steps to help her feel supported in discovering her "new normal." Hopefully they will help you as well with what you are experiencing.

Five Steps to a New Normal

1. *A New Identity*

After your cat has died, your life and daily routines are going to change. You are not the same person that you were when you shared a life with your beloved companion. The normal activities that you had with your cat are gone, and you will have time that you don't know what to do with.

You no longer have a physical relationship with your cat, and there is a possibility that you will have different beliefs and thoughts as a result of your life without your cat.

Your self-identity will naturally change after your cat dies. This was a change that Tracey experienced. People would say to her, "I remember your stories about Luis, the yoga kitty—now what are you going to do?"

This is part of your grief journey and something to keep in mind as your life moves forward without your pal.

2. A New Relationship with Your Cat That Died

Many of my clients in my Rescue Joy from Pet Loss Grief program work on a common goal—to not forget their cat but to change the relationship from a physical presence to one of wonderful memories or to a spiritual relationship.

There are many ways to do this, and the love letter that you wrote in chapter 13 will help you gain a profound connection by thanking your cat for all the wonderful things that they gave you.

By forming your new identity without your cat and allowing yourself to enjoy memories, you will begin to have a new relationship with them that is based on a different type of connection.

In chapter 15, we are going to talk about the afterlife. If you believe in energy connections, I will help you explore ways in which you can connect with your cat on a telepathic level.

3. *A New Group of Friends*

Even though we live in a society that loves its pets, there are some people that don't understand or respect the fact that losing a beloved cat is extremely painful. This could be a difficult time for you because you may feel alone with your grief.

You may find that after your cat dies, your old friends no longer support you because they become impatient with your grief process. Finding new friends that are more supportive of you is extremely important. For example, you may find yourself relying on and investing more time in relationships with people that are most supportive and not with those that are judgmental.

4. *A New Sense of Purpose*

A common feeling that my clients go through is that they question their purpose in life. Tracey did this when Luis died. She actually thought about giving up her yoga practice because she felt like Luis was a vital part of how she processed her postures. She didn't think she could do it alone.

Like Tracey, your cat made a difference in your life, and you depended on each other for happiness and companionship. Your cat helped you shape your daily routine and also played a crucial role in transforming your living space into a comfortable, special home. Now that your cat has died, you may be questioning the meaning of your current existence. This is common and understandable.

Some people realize new life purposes and make significant life changes after their cats have died. For example, some decide to volunteer at local humane societies, start cat rescue groups of their own, or, like Tracey, spend time learning about how their deceased cat can still be part of their life by learning animal communication.

5. *Celebration of Your Growth*

As you experience life without your beloved companion and explore the ways in which your life is changing, your outcome will depend on how you view your new situation.

You didn't choose to experience the loss of your cat. Grief is usually unwanted or unplanned. However, the journey of grief can also be a wonderful experience for personal growth. This type of mourning can be the exact remedy for you to heal your pain.

When you celebrate how you have grown from having shared your heart and soul with your feline companion, it can help you realize the beautiful and rich life that you had with your cat. It can also help you learn how comfortable you can feel in your new normal.

Some of my clients have learned how to be more sensitive to others by living through their own pain from the loss of their cat. Others decide to share their hearts and give back to cats in need. Some learn to celebrate the gifts that their cats gave them and live their lives in completely different ways.

After Tracey worked through these five steps and discovered a different way of dealing with her grief, she was then able to move forward with a different sense of how her life had changed. She eventually began to feel more confident with her unexpected feelings of joy and happiness.

Did Tracey's grief go completely away? No, it did not, but it changed and wasn't as raw.

Tracey shared with me at the end of the Rescue Joy from Pet Loss Grief program, "I never thought I would be able to survive after Luis died. He was my everything. He was my anchor, my purpose, my joy and happiness. When he died, I felt like I didn't deserve to feel these things anymore. But by exploring these five steps on my own time, I was able to realize that what I was feeling was normal and my life was going to be okay."

Tracey's experience helped her understand how important it was to know what to expect. It helped her remember that her grief journey was unique to her and normal. With this knowledge she was able to proceed as she wished with her grief journey.

Unexpected, Powerful Experiences

Here are some unexpected things that Tracey experienced that you may or may not experience after your cat dies.

You may become aware of:

- some different and unexpected changes in your life;

- a time when you really feel the full extent of your loss;

- ways to redefine your relationship with your deceased cat;

- new discoveries of some areas of personal growth through your pet grief; and/or

- the joy you feel when recalling the memories that you shared together with your dear feline pal.

Remember, this can be a very challenging time period for you. The extent of your loss is felt, and new feelings of grief will emerge.

The Emergence of Your New Normal

During this stretch of time, you will begin to recognize how your life is taking on something we can call your "new normal"—the new thoughts, decisions, and changes in your outlook in regard to your life without your cat.

You may move into a phase of discovering your new normal by taking steps that move you towards understanding life without the physical presence of your cat.

You may spend time with new friends, have different adventures, or do things you have always wanted to do but never did.

You may begin to think about getting another cat or volunteering at your local humane society.

You may even have some feelings of relief, which is common to feel and part of the seven stages of grief that you learned about in chapter 2. If your cat was very ill and suffered a lot during the end of their life, you may feel relieved that they died and are no longer suffering. This too is a feeling that most people experience.

If your cat died suddenly or unexpectedly, this could present you with an entirely different experience and process. Be patient as this type of trauma takes time to process, and you may not be ready to discover your new normal yet.

Remember, there are many things that will happen during this stage of pet loss and grief. They will be unique to you, depending on your experience.

Like grief in general, there will be no prescribed timeframe when you experience these feelings or you may not even have these feelings at all. The relationship that you had with your cat is special to the both of you, and that will never change.

Your cat will live in your heart forever. This is a beautiful blessing that is private and special to the both of you. This place in your heart and the lessons that your cat gave your soul will influence how you choose to live with the changes in your life.

Your memories of cuddling on the couch, playing hide-and-seek, and sharing love will never go away. These pictures are part of you now, living and breathing as you do, and contributing to how you look at life and death. How your grief plays out is the perfect remedy to make choices to change your life.

Let me pause a moment to remind you that this doesn't mean that your active grief will change quickly over the days, weeks, months, and years after your cat dies. It doesn't mean that a new normal will begin to develop right away. It can and probably will take its time.

Another feeling that you may begin to recognize is more joy in your life. Please rest assured, it doesn't mean that you will no longer experience grief from the loss of your cat. It just means that you will begin to feel a shift in your awareness in regard to your grief.

When experiencing your new normal, you will be able to continue to acknowledge and honor your grief, which certainly will resurface. This is what grief is about—it has a life of its own. Yet, during this stage, you will be able to recognize and celebrate your growth and gains as well!

No matter what your experience is during this time, continue to believe in your own process and grow with compassion. Your grief is distinctively yours! It will continue to change, so reflect upon what you are going through.

Chapter Wrap-Up

Your new normal is part of the grieving process. By making some changes and experiencing a different type of relationship with your cat, it will never take away the forever bond that you shared with your cat when they were alive.

Please revisit the five steps for discovering your new normal to assist you in dealing with the fact that your cat is no longer physically with you. Each time you review the steps, you will learn, process, and understand something new that can be implemented into your daily journey. Know that you will feel out of place at times, confused, and frustrated—and that is okay.

Your journey with pet grief is unique to you and your cat. Honor your journey with respect and dignity for yourself and your furry companion. No one can alter that if you are aware of and accountable for your process.

Use the chapter's *Contemplation Questions* to help you be prepared for your new normal and the action that you can take to heal your pet grief.

If you believe in energy connections and the afterlife, in chapter 15, I share that you can have a forever bond with your cat. If you believe in the spiritual nature of the universe and that energy is infinite, you will get relief in knowing that even though your cat is not with you physically, they are with you in a nonphysical or spiritual existence.

Chapter 14 Contemplation Questions

1. You learned about some of the ways in which you can expect change in your life—your new normal—after your cat reaches the end of their life. What makes sense to you? What are you going through?

2. Do you have any feelings of joy or happiness due to what you learned from your cat? Do you feel okay with those feelings?

3. What are the ways in which you can be sure you receive the support you need when experiencing your "new normal"?

15. Discovering the Afterlife

You have been learning a lot about your grief, how to say good-bye, and ways to deal with the trauma of losing your cat. Most of this information has been very practical. By articulating your heartfelt affection and your love for the special moments that your relationship with your cat gave you, you will find peace with the feelings, emotions, decisions, and options for healing the trauma of losing your cat.

Another important part of your journey is to consider the spiritual aspect of your relationship with your cat. This subject is huge and will be a book of its own in the near future, but for now, I would like to get you started with understanding some of the things that happen to your cat in the nonphysical world.

An important element to understanding the nonphysical world happens via animal mediumship. What animal or pet mediumship refers to is a person experiencing contact with the energy or spirit of their deceased pet through the guidance and expertise of a medium. The role of a medium is to translate and communicate messages from a pet that has died to the person that shared their life with the pet. Mediums translate messages from the spiritual to the physical realm by hearing, tasting, sensing, feeling, and seeing.

Although a session with an animal medium is not a cure for the grief that you are going through, it can help ease your pain and misery. Receiving information and special messages from your cat in the spiritual realm can assure you that life is eternal.

In my own work as a medium connecting pet owners to their deceased pets, so many people described it as a helpful and reassuring experience. Here is an example of how animal mediumship helped Melanie and her cat, Mister, who were introduced to you in chapter 13.

Case Study — Melanie and Mister

Melanie, Mister, and I had a conversation that was exceedingly healing for Melanie. Since Mister was Melanie's soul kitty, she was distraught that Mister was no longer physically in her life. She felt that Mister left way too soon because there was so much more that Melanie wanted to share with Mister. She was searching for some answers, trying to make sense of her loss and understand her feelings of guilt.

What happened was that I used my animal mediumship skills to establish a communication link with Mister. Through me, Melanie got the opportunity to convey her concerns to Mister, say she was sorry and that she missed him, and listen to Mister's messages back to her.

It was an amazing experience, aiding Melanie in connecting with Mister. Melanie told me that it gave her great solace and the much-needed help she'd been searching for.

It had been a lonely time for Melanie to be without a Mister. So many of her routines were gone, and life had changed. Although Melanie has other cats to share her love with, she was experiencing a terrible void.

Melanie shared, "As I was talking to Mister through Wendy, I felt an overwhelming sense of oneness. Finally, after 7 years of him being away from me, I knew that we were both okay. I had no idea I could be that close to him again. There were so many tears shed during our conversation."

As with Melanie, having this communication through a medium can also help you to mend the pain of loss, so you can process your grief more fully. By understanding the concept of life after death, you can open your heart to a new relationship with your cat that will never end.

By accepting the fact that energy lives forever, you receive much solace. You will know that your relationship with your cat will continue to deepen and grow, just in a different way.

A Perspective on Death

One way to consider death is to explore the notion that it is a pause between living in physical and nonphysical forms. Your cat will continue loving you and being loyal even after they continue to the afterlife in spirit form. This relationship goes beyond obligation.

You may not feel that you are sensitive enough to be aware of your cat's presence right after death, but your cat may make its presence known to you in a quiet and reassuring way.

They can do this by giving you:

- a brief sighting of them out of the corner of your eye or in a cloud formation;

- a glimpse into their life by way of a dream;

- an opportunity to hear them meow or purr; and/or

- a feeling in your heart that they are close to you.

Case Study — Kate and Willa

My client Kate had a beloved cat named Willa that died of cancer. Kate told me, "Willa died in her sleep in May from terminal cancer. I continued to hear and feel her in the house for days after her death. I could feel her brushing my legs at dinnertime, and I could even hear her purr every night at the same time."

At first, Kate felt a mix of fear and excitement that she was having these experiences. Once she understood that Willa wanted to make sure Kate was okay and remind Kate of her loyalty, Kate allowed herself to explore the possibility of being receptive to future messages.

Months later, she emailed me and shared, "Every time I am stressed about work, Willa comes into my dreams and purrs in my ear. I get the sense she is telling me that I am doing okay. This makes me feel so much better."

When Kate first started to work with me, she had many questions about the afterlife. She feared that Willa was disappearing into nothingness. When she understood that death is the juncture between two worlds, a portion of her grief dissipated.

This is not to say you won't feel suddenly desperate or alone at the death of your cat. The silence and stillness of their body can be a traumatic experience and bring up many unexpected emotions. Yet, when you can witness through an energy connection that your cat's body is physically free of pain and suffering, it can help you gain solace by knowing that when they are in spirit, they do not feel pain.

Even knowing this, there are many questions that you may have. I am going to share with you five of the most common questions that I receive from my clients.

Common Questions Concerning the Afterlife

Question #1 – What happens when my cat dies?

When your furry feline companion dies, they move into spiritual energy or existing as a soul spirit. They exist without sickness, pain, or fear. Your cat in energy form is cherished and respected for the work they did with you on Earth, which is extremely honorable. Since they are living in spirit, their role is to prepare and transition for their next role.

Right after they die, there is a transition period that can take up to two weeks. This may be the time that you see, feel, hear, and/or sense their presence. Know that it is okay. They are just making the transition in their own way and reminding you they love you.

Question #2 – Why did my cat behave the way they did before dying?

If your cat exhibited any new behaviors days, hours, or minutes before dying, this was their way of transitioning their energy. There will be a period of time when they are in-between bodies, which means they are partly in the physical form and they haven't quite made the full transition into death or the spiritual form.

Question #3 – Does my cat that died have a special message for me?

The answer is YES! When a cat dies, they are still contactable and often want to continue to contact their people for many years. Even though they are not in the physical body, their spirit is alive and well. You can still see, hear, or sense your cat, even if for a fleeting moment.

When they do contact you, there is purpose in that connection, so having an animal medium help you sort out this message can be helpful. You can consider your cat as your lifetime guide or guru, helping you to find peace amongst the chaos of being human.

Question #4 – Will my cat come back to live with me?

They can and they do! They will come back as an animal companion. Animals do not reincarnate as humans.

Also, parts of their "personality" can also come back as part of another pet's personality.

A cat named Cassy definitely came back to Sally years later after Cassy went to the afterlife. Sally got a new kitten from her local humane society. She named her Banjo and as Banjo grew and developed her personality over a few months, Sally started noticing very similar traits to Cassy's, like using her paw to drink water while lying down. Sally had many cats, and Cassy and Banjo were the only kitties that had this behavior.

Question #5 – Does my cat know that they are going to die?

Yes, they do! Cats are fine-tuned and highly evolved beings. They are part of the divine plan to help us be better human beings. They are okay with death, so when they die, it means that their work with us is complete, according to their Earth plan, and that they taught us what we needed to know.

Even though your cat knew they were going to die and entered into a new soul-spirit life, they are always accessible to you. By quieting your soul or spirit, you will be able to contact them and hear what they have to say. My clients are often calmed and relieved when they get their special messages from their dear animal friends.

Chapter Wrap-Up

Connecting with your cat in the afterlife is a healthy way to cope with your grief. Listening to what your cat has to say in spirit form will strengthen your forever bond in a new way.

If you are having a difficult time with the fact that your cat is no longer physically with you, please revisit the five steps to discovering your "new normal" in chapter 14 and consider doing an animal mediumship session to get some answers to your questions. This will help you feel comfortable with this stage of healing.

Your journey with the loss of your cat is unique to you and your cat. Although your cat is now in spirit form, they are still reachable. You can do this on your own or with the help of an animal medium.

Here are your final *Contemplation Questions* to help you explore the option of connecting with your cat in the afterlife. Dedicate yourself to these questions only if you believe in this concept or only when you are ready.

Chapter 15 Contemplation Questions

1. What are your experiences of "sensing" your cat's presence?

2. Have you had any dreams of your cat? What do you think is the message your cat wants to share with you through the dream?

3. How are you still spiritually connected to your cat?

Final Thoughts

You and your cat shared an incredible life together. These times were special occasions for you that you will always cherish and hold in your heart. You experienced many escapades, joys, and adventures that will continue to help you understand all that life with a cat has to offer.

Together you gave each other an incredible sense of belonging, purpose, and joy. Your cat connected you to other animals, people, nature, the universe, and new ways of looking at life. Their ability to listen, teach, and heal was acquired when you listened to them and acted upon the lessons they showed and shared with you.

Your cat gave you stability when you couldn't get that from family, friends, and co-workers. Together you made each other's life full of purpose, a little easier, and much more fun.

Learning about living life in the present and freeing the soul to experience happiness is what your cat excelled in. They never wavered from this. Your cat constantly reminded you to never give up on yourself and that you are awesome. Your cat taught you to spend your valuable time with people and adventures that matter most.

The daily conversations that you had with your cat were profound, life-changing, and sometimes silly. Your cat had the uncanny ability to help you see things for what they truly were. Your cat changed your outlook on life.

Without judgment, complaint, or impatience, your cat listened to your secrets that many a human being would never consider doing or will never know about you. The confidentiality that you shared with your cat was your special pact, a special bond not to be accessed by any other living being.

It is, therefore, your right to feel raw, angry, sad, depressed, etc., now that your cat has died and they are no longer snuggled by your side. This unavoidable event that ultimately happens in every cat-lover's life is mind-crushing and heart-splitting. And some people just don't understand. When your cat is ripped from your life, you can expect changes and some not all that comfortable.

You can expect that you are going to feel chaotic, isolated, irritated, ravenous, perplexed, bewildered, mixed-up, and all the other normal and common feelings of grief.

In order to soothe your soul, keep in mind that your bond with your cat was not shared by anyone else. It was entirely exclusive and exceptional to the two of you. Therefore, what you experience is going to reflect your personality, your cat's personality, and all the things that you shared together.

Your job now is to mourn and experience the changes in your life without your beloved feline. Learn from them and ultimately fill your heart again with the joy that is now lost.

You are going to experience that some people are just not going to get what you are going through and will encourage you to move on before you are ready. That is okay. It is not your job to change their opinions. Turn your attention to your memories and your cat.

Be ready for the fact that you will be faced with some tough and annoying decisions that will demand your attention, and that is what you can spend your valuable energy on to fully process your loss. You want to be able to make these decisions without regret, guilt, or remorse.

The important thing to do is to get in touch with your feelings of grief and learn how they are going to help you throughout your life. Do not allow the non-believers to take your beautiful memories from your heart.

Mourn your emotions and celebrate the life of your cat with supportive and non-judgmental friends, family, support groups, or a pet loss coach. Through this experience, you are going to find a remedy for your personal pain by taking care of yourself, your beliefs, and the gifts that you received from your cat.

Your life purpose and journey will not end now that your cat has died. Instead, you will gain some incredible insight that will split your heart open to receive a continued relationship with your cherished feline on a spiritual level if you so choose. Your life will be enriched and soulfully balanced.

The changes you are experiencing and your feelings of being lost without your feline companion result in a tremendous impact in the way you are now moving through life. This book took you by the hand and supported you with tools and options on how you can walk this part of your pet loss voyage with a warm heart and a gentle nudge. I hope you took me up on my offer of the free, downloadable Healing Cat Loss

Meditation.mp3. By engaging in this short meditation, daily or even a few times a week, you will soften the rough patches of your journey of grief.

With my program Rescue Joy from Pet Loss Grief, which is your next step after this book, you can continue to receive support as you continue the journey. This time-tested program that has already helped many others has been created with you in mind to bring you wisdom and personal growth, so you can reach a place of profound understanding that is different from what you are experiencing now. If you would like to experience support on this level, please go to the resources section to contact me.

Stephanie, who lost her beautiful calico Anja, explained the Rescue Joy from Pet Loss Grief program in this way:

Without this program, I couldn't have understood the crazy feelings that I was having that kept me from functioning in my daily life. What it did for me was give me tools, help, hope, and strength to keep going and not give up. I was able to focus on my grief, mourn, and see that I could continue having a relationship with Anja even though she had died. Without this program, I would have been focusing on all the stuff that would keep me believing all the negative myths that society expects us to believe about life, death, and the afterlife. Wendy and her course helped me experience and trust my knowledge, intuition, and process.

Like Stephanie, trust that your ultimate journey is a reflection of what you experienced and what you are experiencing now. The life you had while your cat was physically with you will give you the inspiration and accountability to develop a different connection with your cat that will last your lifetime.

When you are ready to celebrate your cat with a pet funeral, memorial, or celebration-of-life ceremony, you will be actively making a commitment to your cat and recognizing them as an integral part of your life, family, and personal growth. Your cat was your best friend, and you are healthy to mourn their loss by creating a special service of celebration.

When you celebrate the special memories that you shared with your cat, it will help you experience your grief in a healthy way.

Resources

Ways in which I can support you

Center for Pet Loss Grief: Through Life, Death, and Beyond
Wendy Van de Poll, MS, CEOL

https://centerforpetlossgrief.com

Best Selling and Award Winning Books
https://centerforpetlossgrief.com/books

My Dog IS Dying: What Do I Do?
My Dog HAS Died: What Do I Do?

My Cat IS Dying: What Do I Do?
My Cat HAS Died: What Do I Do?

Healing A Child's Pet Loss Grief

Free Book
Healing Your Heart From Pet Loss Grief

Free Pet Grief Support Kit
https://centerforpetlossgrief.com

Animal Mediumship
https://centerforpetlossgrief.com/animal-medium

Animal Communication
https://wendyvandepoll.com/animal-communication

Pet Funerals
https://centerforpetlossgrief.com/pet-funeral

Facebook
Center for Pet Loss Grief
https://facebook.com/centerforpetlossgrief

Pet Memorial Support Group
https://facebook.com/groups/petmemorials.
centerforpetlossgrief

Veterinarians:

Veterinary Medical Association
www.ahvma.org/

Home Euthanasia and Pet Hospice Veterinarians
www.iaahpc.org/

Online Product Support:

Herbal Support: Pet Wellness Blends Affiliate
www.herbs-for-life-3.myshopify.com/#_l_1e

Magnetic Therapy Supplies: aVivoPur Affiliate
www.avivopur.com/#_a_CenterForPetLossGrief

Heart in Diamonds: Affiliate
www.heart-in-diamonds.com/?aff=CenterForPetLoss

Support Groups:

Association for Pet Loss and Bereavement
www.aplb.org/

International Association for Animal Hospice and Palliative Care
www.iaahpc.org/

Association for Human-Animal Bond Veterinarians
www.aahabv.org/

Another book on Pet Loss by Wendy Van de Poll, MS, CEOL

Healing A Child's Pet Loss Grief

A Guide for Parents

Are you a parent of a child who is facing the loss of their pet and would like to support your child during this difficult time?

Are you really worried about your child feeling depressed, alone, or confused when their pet dies?

Do you know how to show your child how to view your pet as a compassionate teacher of pet loss and the cycle of life?

Healing a Child's Pet Loss Grief: A Guide for Parents has been written for parents who are looking for a no-nonsense approach to teach their child about life, death, and beyond in an easy and concise manner. This book guides parents from the day they begin to think about getting a pet to when the family pet reaches the end of life and parents want to help their child manage the loss.

If you are a parent of a child between the ages of 6 and 12, then *Healing a Child's Pet Loss Grief: A Guide for Parents* will act as your close friend, confidant, and mentor to guide you so that you can support your child on how to care for the new family pet and how to manage their grief once the family pet dies.

Family pets make the best teachers for children, instructing them about responsibility, compassion, and, eventually, grief and loss. With this book's guidance, parents can be sure that their children recognize and act on those valuable lessons that family pets impart. *Healing a Child's Pet Loss Grief* guides parents in doing just that! You will find practical tools, case studies, and Action Planning Steps in each chapter to guide you on:

- How to choose the right pet for your lifestyle and your child

- How to introduce a new pet into your home and to your child

- How to recognize opportunities when your pet is trying to teach your child valuable lessons; and how to support your child in learning those valuable lessons that your pet is teaching

- How to help your child express and manage their grief once your beloved family pet dies

A family pet can bring your family closer together by teaching about life, death, and how death is not to be feared.

Be the family that steers your child to view the family pet as a compassionate teacher of love, responsibility, joy, loss, and healing. Teaching children early in their lives to recognize the cycle of life and not fear death helps them as adults to be more grounded in their own feelings and to be more compassionate and respectful towards all living creatures as a whole.

This book will help you and your family create a compassionate, respectful, healthy, and loving journey for your child and the family pet—from the time you consider introducing a pet to your family to when your beloved family pet dies and your child is distraught.

Remember, your child does not need to feel alone with pet loss and confused by death! And neither do you!

To receive notification when this book is published, please go to www.centerforpetlossgrief.com, and we'll include you on the mailing list after you download your free gift.

Acknowledgments

First, I would love to express my deepest compassion to all of my clients and readers who feel safe with walking the challenging journey of healing pet loss without questioning the fact that there is life after death.

My sentiment and responsiveness goes to the stories of Kris and Lily, Melissa and Ra, Sandi and Foxtail, Jannie and White Paws, Maggie and Fred, Tara and Puddles, Ellen and Twinkles, Theresa and River, Amy and Patches, Patsy and Popcorn, Victoria and Zen-ne, Sahara, Zach, and Gilbert, Joanne, Mike, Jason, and Beeker, Angel and Apricot, Azia and Curry, Lucy and Shadow, Carol, Hans, and Tigger, Tracey and Luis, Sally and Banjo, Stephanie and Anja, Kate and Willa, Chris and Pudding, and Melanie and Mister.

To Nick the Cat, who graciously accepted the job of a potential modeling career for the cover of this book. But Nick tired quickly of his potential new mission in life. He chose managing his backyard chipmunks instead.

I would also like to shout out to the folks at Self-Publishing School that have guided me to follow my lifelong passion of becoming a bestselling author. My SPS family and my launch team members are the best!

I am truly in awe of my editor, Nancy Pile, who once again added her heart and paws to bring my book to another level.

Thank you to Debbie Lum for her beautiful formatting, and to Danijela Mijailovic for her gorgeous book cover artistry.

To Addie, Marley, Kado, Maya, and the rest of my fur, feather, and fin gurus who continue to hold my heart through vital life lessons and goals that I am determined to accomplish. They are amazing and wise teachers. They never let me forget who I am.

My super-human husband Rick! Your dedication to me is appreciated and loved with every cell of my body.

About the Author

Wendy Van de Poll is a pioneering leader in the field of pet loss grief support. Wendy is dedicated to providing a safe place for her clients to express their grief over the loss of their pets.

What makes Wendy successful with her clients is that she get's grief! *"Over the years I've dealt with my own grief and helping many families communicate and connect with their pets long after their loss. It's what I've done since I was just 5 yrs old!"*

She is compassionate and supportive to all who know her.

Her passion is to help people when they are grieving over the loss of a pet and her larger than life love for animals has led her to devote her life to the mission of increasing the quality of life between animals and people no matter what stage they are in their cycle of life! She has been called the animal whisperer.

She is a Certified End of Life and Pet Grief Support Coach, Certified Pet Funeral Celebrant, Animal Medium and Communicator. She is the founder of The Center for Pet Loss Grief and an international best selling and award-winning author and speaker.

She holds a Master's of Science degree in Wolf Ecology and Behavior and has run with wild wolves in Minnesota, coyotes in Massachusetts and foxes in her backyard. She lives in the woods with her husband, two crazy birds, her rescue dog Addie and all kinds of wildlife.

Wendy currently has a Skype, phone, and in person practice, providing end-of-life and pet grief support coaching, gentle massage and energy healing for animals, animal mediumship, and personalized pet funerals.

You can reach her at www.centerforpetlossgrief.com.

Thank You for Reading

My Cat Has Died: What Do I Do?
Making Decisions and Healing the Trauma of Pet Loss

Hi, my name is Mister, or Magic, as my mom, Melanie, liked
to call me. As you can see, I am a very beautiful cat. I am sure
you can tell I am very wise just by looking in my eyes! Since
this book is dedicated to rescue cats all over the world that
have yet to find their soul-peeps, it would mean a lot if you

left a review on Amazon because Wendy, the author, really gets us, animals, and always has our backs.

When I came to live with Melanie, Melanie didn't know it yet, but I had a divine plan for her. I gave her a ton of unconditional love when her heart was raw. I got to heal her from the inside out.

My goal for this book is to help Wendy support you and show you how to heal your heart, allowing it to mend. With patience, love, and respect your journey will be softer. As a rescue cat, I know that really well!

I loved that my mom asked Wendy to talk to me in spirit and that Wendy wrote this book to help you on your grieving journey. I would be grateful if you would leave a helpful REVIEW on Amazon.

Please go to this link: www.amzn.com/B01L5UW5MY to Leave Your Review.

Thank you,

Mister

The Pet Bereavement Series
Best Selling and Award Winning Books

By Wendy Van de Poll, MS, CEOL

My Dog IS Dying: What Do I Do?
My Dog HAS Died: What Do I Do?

My Cat IS Dying: What Do I Do?
My Cat HAS Died: What Do I Do?

Healing A Child's Pet Loss Grief

Free Book

Healing Your Heart From Pet Loss Grief

Made in United States
North Haven, CT
15 December 2022